CREATE YOUR OWN
STAGE PRODUCTION COMPANY
Gill Davies

CREATE YOUR OWN
STAGE PRODUCTION COMPANY
Gill Davies

Back Stage Books
an imprint of Watson-Guptill Publications
New York

First published 2000 by
Back Stage Books, an imprint of
Watson-Guptill Publications
BPI Communications
770 Broadway
New York
NY 10003
USA

ISBN 0-8230-7714-4

Published simultaneously in the UK by
A & C Black (Publishers) Limited
35 Bedford Row
London WC1R 4JH

Create Your Own Stage Effects
was conceived, edited and designed by
Playne Books Limited
Chapel House
Trefin, Haverfordwest
Pembrokeshire SA62 5AU
United Kingdom

Editor
Vivienne Kay

Research and editorial assistant
Faye Hayes

Designers and illustrators
Richard Cotton
Jonathan Douglas
Craig John
David Playne

Typeset by Playne Books Limited
in Glypha

Printed in Hong Kong

Contents

Contents

Contents

Contents

Contents

About this book

Following on the other highly successful titles in the *Create Your Own* stage series, this latest title aims to help theatre groups, schools, colleges, and any other enthusiasts, whether amateur or semi-professional, to create their own theatre company or to make their existing one far more efficient and successful.

While many books concentrate on the technical aspects of theatre, the aim here is to cover the organisation and administration – the planning and management that is such a vital element in any good theatre group. The book provides a careful analysis of everything that needs to be done, from the finding of the right script to the clearing up after the last performance.

To provide practical help, the book includes a range of blank forms, such as advance booking forms, audition sheets and so on. These pages have been cleared of copyright restrictions so they can be photocopied and used by the readers. In addition, there are also many checklists, cue sheets, step-by-step guidelines and hints and tips on many different aspects of production.

The aim here is to assist and improve planning, organisation and production. For full technical know-how, readers will need to explore the wealth of books that specialise in these areas of expertise, together with the other titles in this *Create Your Own* series!

While any new theatre group will find this book an enormous asset to their enterprise, existing societies will also be helped enormously by the clear, informative analysis and the ready-made lists and forms. In effect, the book should enable any drama organisation, however small or large, new or old, to achieve a smooth-running production and to channel their enthusiasm efficiently.

Introduction

Creating a show is an exciting enterprise. The launch of any new production will be fired with fresh enthusiasm and energy. Unfortunately, this initial positive spirit will soon be undermined if there is poor organisation. Anyone who has gulped down, or entirely by-passed, a meal to make a rehearsal on time – only to find out that they are not needed – will be aware of the importance of good communication. And the fury of the costumes department, who have slaved to create an outfit to fit a slim actress when the casting has changed and passed on the role to somebody three sizes larger, knows no bounds!

Maintaining a happy, committed team means keeping everybody fully informed.

Every group – and every play – needs a solid structure and good planning.

There is no point in rehearsing for many weeks on end only to discover that the chosen play is not actually available for production at this point in time or that the venue needs to undergo major building works to meet fire regulations.

There is a good deal of 'red tape' to be undertaken before and during the production. Meanwhile, both auditions and rehearsals must be well structured, the technical aspects planned, back stage and front-of-house teams organised, publicity and ticket sales set in motion, the programmes, tickets and posters created, and sensible budgets set up and maintained.

However, it is certainly worth taking up the challenge, for, when handled efficiently, a good production is one of the most satisfying undertakings in which to participate. The glow of pleasure when a show is well received and the audience applause rings in your ears takes a lot of beating! Even the smallest company with a limited budget can achieve great stage success.... So give every production that extra edge and confidence that is made possible by hard work and competent forward thinking. Then your production team, your cast and, ultimately, your audience will be happy!

Good luck!

Gill Davies

How to begin

Two kinds of launch

There are two 'how to begin's. The first 'how to begin' is how to set a up a new society – how to launch a new group. The second 'how to begin' refers to starting a new production but within an established company.

Much of the production organisation and protocol will remain the same in both. A new 'raw' company and an established theatre group both need to set in place careful planning, checklists and a structured discipline so that the play has the best possible start in life.

Pages 24-31 in *Organisation and 'red tape'* describe a good deal of the practical organisation and 'nitty-gritty' of red tape that every group must address. The aim in this section is to look at how to muster the necessary support, share the workload and find a suitable script and venue.

New groups

There is something especially exciting about a first production for a new group. The 'high' that follows a success is even more exhilarating when this is the first play that the group has performed.

However, before this point is reached, there will be many moments during the course of the production when the group will wonder if they will ever achieve their dream. There is so much to do and organise. To the uninitiated, this may seem almost overwhelming. There is great fear that something vital may be overlooked or not remembered until very late in the day – by which time panic sets in.

The aim of this entire book is to help

overcome this problem, to arm the company with all the checklists and the guidelines needed for a smooth-running organisation, and ultimately, a successful show.

How to start up a new group

Gathering a team

Initiating a drama group is no mean task. The decision to put on a production may be one person's dream; or it

may be the result of several friends' shared enthusiasm for the idea. Now it is time to drum up sufficient support, to find a team that is capable of putting on a show and turning the vision into reality.

There are various ways to begin

Word of mouth
Personal enthusiasm remains the best 'draw'. Talk to everyone you meet about your aims and the excitement

of this new venture. Talk to all the members of all your families. Telephone all your friends. The word will spread surprisingly quickly.

Advertising
Use whatever means are available to advertise what is happening and attract further members to your new theatre group.

Where and how to to advertise

1
Posters displayed around the area

2
Inserts in local newsletters or the local Press

3
Advertisements on notice boards

4
Announcements in schools and colleges

5
Coverage in local amateur dramatic journals

6
Information hand-outs:
these may be left in
local shops and
libraries
or
posted through letterboxes

Other groups
Talk to other societies and companies. They may be willing to advise or offer practical help. They might know interested people who have moved into your area. If you are very lucky, they may even 'loan' personnel if they are between productions.

How many people are required?

A society can be formed by just two or three people, if they are willing to commit huge chunks of their time. Many new groups begin this way, in fact, with a hard-core team doing a little of everything! However, the more the workload can be spread and specific roles undertaken by different individuals, the easier it will become to achieve a successful, smooth production: a one-man band will make music but can never sound the same as a full orchestra!

The minimum quantity is the number of the cast (with doubling up as required), at least one technical body to control lighting and sound, plus the front of house team. If the team is very small, cast members can undertake much of the pre-performance backstage work. They can certainly create scenery and costumes, collect properties, sell tickets, make the tickets and programmes, and so on. One may even direct.

During performances, however, it can be very difficult to concentrate properly on acting a role if your energies are also required to shift scenery, find properties, draw the curtain – or even prompt – between appearances. The more backstage help that can be called upon, the easier it will be for all concerned – so try to build as strong a support team as possible.

Often actors' partners or family can be persuaded to help behind the scenes. As a guide to an ideal formula, the various backstage roles will be found in the list on page 23.

Meanwhile, a well organised front of house team will be essential to control the sale of tickets, programmes, seating and so on in the auditorium.

Funding a new group

To stage a production costs quite a substantial sum of money. Generally, the more professional the end result,

Funds can be raised in the following ways:

1
Each member makes a financial contribution. This may take the form of a joining fee

2
Each member lends the group an advance that will be refunded after the production (or several productions) has created a profit

3
Fund-raising activities are held first, to raise sufficient capital. These might be fêtes, rummage sales, raffles, disco nights, competitions, or whatever

4
Local companies are invited to sponsor the production

5
Grants may be available, especially if children or young people are involved in the company; make enquiries – local councils and advisory groups may be able to advise (see also pages 22 and 112)

You can also:

6
Ask local companies to advertise in the programme and charge them for this

7
Ask friends and colleagues if they would like to become founder patrons of the group and be charged a rational fee for the honour!

New groups

especially on the technical side, the more that needs to be spent.

However, a new group usually begins with an empty 'kitty'. It may take a while to build up a respectable sum, sufficient to launch a full-scale show prior to ticket sale revenue arriving.

During the performances, more funds can be raised by holding raffles, selling T-shirts, sweatshirts, badges, toys and other such items, preferably personalised to the group or to the particular production.

Cost-cutting

THE AVENING PLAYERS

BEAU VEST 1985

TREASURE SPYLAND 1986

HOP-ALONG DICK TWITTINGTON 1987

LITTLE AVENING BY THE SEA 1988

SHERBERT FOREST 1989

WOK'S IT ALL ABOUT ALADDIN! 1990

BILLY BANDEEGO'S FANTASTIC MAGIC FAIR 1991

THE SCARLET WIMPERNEL 1992

MURDER, MYSTERY AND SUSPENDERS 1993

MONOPOLY 1994

NEVER CLIMB A BEANSTALK! 1995

RAPUNZEL 1996

CINDERS IN ORBIT 1997

Big Bad Wolf 1998

Rumpelstiltskin 1999

Snow White and the seven tall dwarfs 2000

Selling T-shirts or sweatshirts dedicated to the group can help to raise funds. A list of previous productions works well

---

To keep down costs, the following economies may help:

1
Beg or borrow lighting and sound equipment, rather than hiring

2
Find fabric for costumes in rummage sales

3
See if local carpenters, builders or suppliers can contribute left-over timber, board, expanded polystyrene or the like for the sets and properties – remember to thank them in the programme

4
Choose a play that is 'out of copyright' or write your own

5
Try to negotiate special 'first-time' rates at your venue. Rehearsals may need to take

---

place elsewhere if charges are high. In this case, approach members with large lounges; try public houses (inns), school halls or gymnasiums, social clubs, church halls, meeting rooms and so on.

If a piano accompaniment is necessary but the rehearsal venue is without, recording the music on tape can alleviate the need for the pianist to play at every rehearsal

Also check out if anyone can help with the photocopying of home-produced scripts, programmes, posters and so on

---

Ask the group members to contribute:

1
Old curtains and bedcovers as a source of fabrics for costumes

2
Raffle prizes

3
Properties

4
Furniture for sets

5
Left-over household paint (not gloss) for the scenery

6
Unwanted items of make-up and/or ask them to bring their own personal make-up

7
Boxes of tissues and toilet paper for make-up removal

8
Cardboard or plastic boxes for storage

Attracting an audience

Publicity (pages 104-119) describes the conventions of theatre promotion, but a new group will have to work extra hard to raise their first audience. After a successful and enjoyable production, many audience members will continue to support the group – but persuading them to leave their armchairs and television sets for the first ever show requires grim determination – cloaked under oodles of enthusiastic noises.

New groups do arouse curiosity so capitalise on this. Any person who makes polite enquiries about the 'goings-on' may be a potential ticket purchaser. Never be afraid to ask anyone to support you, however unlikely a candidate he or she might seem!

Establishing the group as an entity

As well as putting on the first show, the new group will need to be recognised in order to 'exist' officially.

The following formalities must be addressed:

1
The group should have a name

2
It needs a postal address

3
It will need a secretary

4
A full committeee may be established, with a constitution and various officers, including a chairman, secretary and treasurer

5
An auditor may need to be appointed to oversee all the accounts

6
The group will need a bank account and a cheque book, with agreed signatories

7
The group's name and address should be sent to regional drama organisers and to any other appropriate holders of listings and directories

Old curtains and household fabrics are a source of material for costumes

Venues

Many groups are formed within colleges, schools, cities, towns and villages, within church groups or other societies where there is an existing hall or performance area. Even when life is this simple, there are various factors to consider and the venue should be looked over carefully before planning the appropriate staging, sets and moves.

Assessing the venue

You will need to examine:

1 The stage area: measure this carefully. You will need to know its dimensions when plotting moves and planning sets. Is an extension required? If there is no stage at all, will you manage without, perform 'in the round' – or can anyone point you in the right direction to find stage blocks or to build a temporary platform?

2 How can entrances and exits be effected? For example do wings, legs or tabs exist or must these be constructed? Are any steps up to the stage required?

3 Is there a grid above the stage or any means of flying scenery?

4 Is audience seating available or must this be borrowed or hired?

5 Is lighting equipment part of the facilities? If not, what structures exist for the rigging of lights?

6 You will need to assess the audience capacity.

7 How many toilets are available? Are these sufficient for the size of the audience planned plus the cast

Venues

and all the production team?

8 Are there any changing rooms – and a suitable place to do make-up? If not, can these be constructed somehow?

9 Are there facilities for catering?

10 Are there fire exits and signs? (see also page 24.)

11 Is the building sound and safe?

12 Are there storage facilities available for costumes, properties and scenery? If not, what are the alternatives?

Never simply assume that this venue will be available for the new group. Make enquiries immediately. Apart from the fact that such places are often booked up early, there is inevitably a certain protocol involved over who can use it – when and how – and it is all too easy to upset those in charge by not following the correct procedure.

Other venues

It may be that there is no obvious venue available, or perhaps the usual venue may be already booked or might have become too expensive. It may be that, for all sorts of reasons, the group want a change of scene. For example, a production with a religious theme can work very well in a church or chapel, and Shakespeare lends itself to open-air theatre. The group may be 'going on tour', taking the show to another society's venue, entering a festival, or trying street the-

atre. It can be refreshing to perform somewhere different, and the change may inspire new thinking and an invigorated approach.

If the group is new and without a home, needs a different venue to rehearse, or is an established group that suddenly has to look elsewhere, the members might consider the following and see if any of these are available or appropriate:

Schools

Sports halls

Churches and chapels

Libraries

Local scout halls, village halls, or the like

Inns and public houses, social clubs

Museums and art galleries

A suitable large house or home might be privately owned or being used as a residential home of some kind, say, for the elderly. Such places often have a large hall 'going begging' but it may take courage to ask!

A barn or other farm buildings

Borrowing someone else's theatre: this might be another local group's venue or a professional theatre or cinema that is available for hire

Converting another building or erecting a purpose-built theatre. Creating a new theatre is a long-term and fairly daunting undertaking but can be highly successful, if funds can be raised. Grants may be available

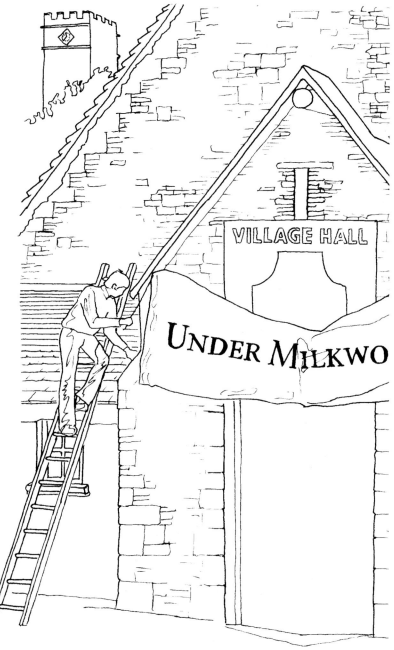

As with attracting a cast or audience, spread the word, ask around, tap into the 'grapevine'.

A determined positive attitude will generally reap rewards.

Whatever the venue, it will need to be looked at carefully as soon as possible as described under *Assessing the venue* on page 15. Then set out to make the most of the site and its particular features.

Scripts

The script is the starting point of any production. It is the raw material that will be developed and moulded, dressed, set, and enacted as the group choose. It must meet the specific needs of the group at this particular point of time.

Choice of play

Generally, groups try to provide a range of entertainment though they may be better at some forms of play than others. Some societies are superb at farces, others at musicals, some at pantomime, some at Shakespeare – and so on. While supporting this 'speciality', most do try to vary the kind of production, to create a balance through the season.

Who selects the play?

1
Generally the selection of the play falls to the producer – upon whose enthusiasm the success of the end-product will depend. A single play or a short-list may be suggested. Generally, this will need to be agreed by a committee

2
Sometimes, the society as a whole, or a committee representing them, makes the choice. A producer can then be invited to take the production forward

3
Several producers may propose potential plays, from which one (plus its producer) will ultimately be chosen

There are practical as well as aesthetic reasons for aiming at variety

1
Certain styles of play – lavish musicals, for example, require tremendous resources and mounting a complicated, demanding show may be possible only once a year

2
Some kinds of play are inevitably more popular than others. They will attract greater audiences and make more money for the group. When an injection of cash is needed, a popular style of production will be preferable

3
There may be several directors or producers, each of whom favours a particular genre

4
The group may wish to capitalise upon the strengths or special skills of certain actors when these particular people are available

What are you looking for?

Reading a script and visualising how the play will work in performance is not always easy. Some people are better at this than others. It is difficult to create the entire picture in your mind's eye from the written page. Humour, especially, is not always immediately obvious.

A reading with other members of the team helps but, even then, the purely visual elements, which will add a lot to the final show, can be overlooked. Read the stage directions. Try to 'see' the play as well as listening to it.

Practical matters will also need to be considered. Inevitably there will be certain restrictions, depending on the venue and the size of the group.

Size of cast

The size of the cast is a major consideration. Try to find a play where the list of characters relates to resources. New members may be profitably drafted in to make the play possible but do not stretch this too far.

However, remember that an apparently large cast list can be misleading. It is not always possible to tell from the brief résumé in a play description how easy it is for characters to be 'doubled up'. An energetic cast can thoroughly enjoy taking several roles.

It means less 'waiting around' during rehearsals – and performances. There are, of course, certain limitations. What seems rational in rehearsal can become a nightmare when the play speeds up in performance. Bear in mind the energies, agility and temperament of the actors concerned before demanding too many rapid-fire costume changes.

Analysing the roles

Put male and female characters into separate columns. Then do the same for the available cast. At this stage, you will not know exactly who is available as play selection must precede the casting. Moreover, the availability or otherwise often depends on whether or not the actors actually like the play, want to be involved at this time and also whether they relish the particular part offered.

Scripts

Scripts may be listed under the following categories

Number of Acts

Type: For example, Comedies, Drama, Serious, The Classics, Costume plays, Mystery and suspense, Musicals, Plays with music, Pantomime, Supernatural, Religious

Setting: For example, Courtroom, Military, Hospital, Convent, School, Shop, Rural

Period: For example, Ancient Rome, Tudor, Georgian, Regency, Victorian, 1920s, Modern

All male/All female

Number of characters and sex: For example, M3 F6

Nation: For example, American, French, Irish

Author(s)

To help strike the right balance and adjust a script to suit the acting force, parts can be subjected to a sex change – especially peripheral roles. With suitable script amendments, a housekeeper can become a butler or an old uncle an ancient aunt.

Inanimate objects and animals in children's shows can, of course, be played by either sex (or both – one at each end) so there is room for further adjustment here too. When making decisions about the choice of play, such parts should be kept in a separate column and then individual characters slipped into the male or female columns as appropriate in the final decision making.

Aim to keep the options open, not to be too ambitious in terms of numbers but to bear in mind that more than one role can be played by a single actor – and some can be tailored to suit your needs. Also, a larger cast means less disappointment amongst those who might otherwise not be given a chance to perform.

Ensure that you do not have to entirely deplete the back-stage team in order to cast!

Love For Love William Congreve *Dramatis Personae*

Men

SIR SAMPSON LEGEND, father to Valentine and Ben	Mr. Underhill
VALENTINE, fallen under his father's displeasure by his expensive way of living, in love with Angelica	Mr. Betterton
SCANDAL, his friend, a free speaker	Mr. Smith
TATTLE, a half-witted beau, vain of his amours, yet valuing himself for secrecy	Mr. Bowman
BEN, Sir Sampson's younger son, half home-bred, and half sea-bred, designed to marry Miss Prue	Mr. Dogget
FORESIGHT, an illiterate old fellow, peevish and positive, superstitious, and pretending to understand astrology, palmistry, physiognomy, omens, dreams, etc., uncle to Angelica	Mr. Sandford
JEREMY, servant to Valentine	Mr. Bowen
TRAPLAND, a scrivener	Mr. Triffusis
BUCKRAM, a lawyer	Mr. Freeman

Women

ANGELICA, niece to Foresight, of a considerable fortune in her own hands	Mrs. Bracegirdle
MRS. FORESIGHT, second wife to Foresight	Mrs. Bowman
MRS. FRAIL, sister to Mrs. Foresight, a woman of the town	Mrs. Barry
MISS PRUE, daughter to Foresight by a former wife, a silly, awkward, country girl	Mrs. Ayliff
NURSE to Miss (Prue)	Mrs. Leigh
JENNY, maid to Angelica	Mrs. Lawson

A STEWARD, OFFICERS, SAILORS, AND SEVERAL SERVANTS

The Scene: in London

Scripts

Other considerations

Age group:
While make-up can, of course, be used to great effect, it is helpful if at least some members of the cast bear a passing resemblance to the ages of the characters.

Decide if children are to be included. They require a good deal of organising, both in rehearsal and during performances.

Music:
Obviously, a complicated musical score requires appropriately skilled interpretation but, equally, it is a shame to rule out musical productions without first checking out the available talent. You may be surprised to discover a rich source of singers and musicians in your midst.

Technical considerations

The technical requirements of production are dealt with in detail in pages 52-85. However, certain elements must be considered at this stage, before choosing and/or adapting a script.

Obviously, if the whole plot depends upon having a revolving stage while your stage consists of blocks at the end of the village hall – then the script will need to be scrutinised carefully to see if it can be translated without being emasculated.

There are three main options:

1
To buy in a published script that is available for amateur production

2
To write your own

3
To borrow a home-grown script from another local group

Similarly, a complicated sound or lighting plot and pyrotechnics may present some problems if the society has limited equipment and expertise.

Few of these difficulties are insurmountable to an imaginative director and technical team but early planning will be essential so that any extra work can be launched in good time.

Generally, you will find that budget and man hours will be in inverse proportion to each other: if you cannot afford to buy or hire it, you will need to make it! So do not choose a play where the input of energy or cash will be totally out of proportion to resources, time or income!

Sources of scripts

For an initial reading, scripts can be borrowed from local libraries, in particular from music and drama specialist libraries which can be found in most cities and offer the widest choice.

Other local societies might be approached for advice on scripts they have used – and there are lots of advertisements for scripts in stage magazines – both in their major advertising panels and in the classified advertisements. You might also 'surf the net' for useful information.

Single reading copies of potential plays can be obtained from play publishers. Most issue a guide to their available scripts. This usually includes a resume of the plots, the list of sets and characters involved – with brief descriptions of each – and states the number of male and female parts. It also classifies the type of play – classical, comedy, court-room drama and so on. Full acting sets may be purchased later and the licence for

---

When We Are Married
Yorkshire farcical comedy.
J. B. Priestley
M8 (young, middle-age) F7 (young, 20s, middle-age).
A sitting-room.
Fee code M.

Twenty-five years ago, the Helliwells, the Parkers and the Soppitts were married on the same day by the same parson. They gather at the Helliwell home to celebrate their silver wedding. The new chapel organist tells them that he recently met the parson who conducted the triple wedding ceremony - he was not authorized to do so. Pandemonium breaks out when these pillars of society believe they have been living in sin for twenty-five years. Period 1900.
ISBN 0 573 01476 0

Spider's Web
Play. Agatha Christie
M8 (30-50, 60) F2 (30). 1 girl (12). A drawing-room.
Fee code M.

When a murder occurs in Clarissa's drawing-room she suspects young step-daughter Pippa. Things are not helped by the imminent arrival of husband Henry with a VIP in tow who might take a dim view of bodies in the drawing-room. However, by the time Henry gets home, the murderer has been unmasked and all is normal, so normal that Henry is utterly unable to believe Clarissa when she explains exactly why there are no refreshments ready for their honoured guest.
ISBN 0 573 01427 2

performance will also need to be cleared prior to rehearsals so that there is no risk of having to abandon the play once underway. Although featured in a publisher's catalogue, a play may be withdrawn from amateur performance if a professional revival is to be staged.

Writing your own script

This can be an exciting challenge. Many amateur companies produce their own scripts – very successfully. It is probably advisable for novice writers to first exercise their skills on a light-hearted, uncomplicated production such as a music hall night or a children's show.

What are the advantages?

1 Cost

Compiling your own script saves the cost of script purchase and royalties. It is not cheap at all, of course, if man-hours are taken into account – but falls very much into the budget-ver-sus-time rule. The task may be undertaken by one author or, in the case of a revue, shared by several. The scripts will need to be typed and then photocopied, of course, and that must be taken into account and costed as necessary.

2 A custom-made play

The play can be tailored to suit the society in all respects. The number of characters, complications of your particular venue and stage, set limitations, budget, costumes, age range and abilities, and all the technical resources can be taken into account.

Moreover, a tailor-made play provides an ideal opportunity to exploit the particular strengths within the group. This assessment and definition of resources will be a useful exercise.

Castle Crazy by Gill Davies

Plot Outline

ACT ONE

Scene 1
The Battlements
Ghosts hold meeting about plan to scare off tourists now the castle is to be opened to the public.
Scene 2
The Grand Entrance Hall
Family of new owners arrive. Various supernatural incidents. Film company arrive to 'shoot' the opening. Cameraman, Gerald, tries to chat up Kate but she explains her long-standing commitment to her distant cousin, Tony. Tony arrives.
Scene 3
The battlements
Kate is exploring.
She meets ghost, Sir Henry Lorditall and they fall for each other.
Scene 4
The Library
Other ghosts, who have been eaves-dropping on the battlements, decide to help Sir Henry Lorditall and Kate.

ACT TWO
Scene 1
The Great Banqueting Hall

Dinner party: Ghosts keep moving food, pouring drinks over diners etc. Film crew are side-tracked into trying to record supernatural incidents.
Scene 2
The Library
Over port, Gerald tackles Tony about Kate. Incited by the ghosts interfer-ence, they commit to a duel at dawn.
Scene 3
The Gardens at Dawn
Ghosts are 'taking sides'.
Sir Henry Lorditall wants to organise it so that both the suitors are shot. Tony and Gerald arrive to duel. Kate has rushed out to stop them but is waylaid by ghosts and an early party of tourists trying to 'beat the rush' who then wander into duel, creating even more havoc. Weapons abandoned, Gerald and Tony become great buddies and decide to transfer their interest to two of the ghosts, Lady Hasitall and Mistress Easy, instead of Kate.
Scene 4
The Maze
Kate meets Sir Henry Lorditall and they 'plight their troth'. All the others arrive to celebrate but there is general hilarity as, to begin with, they cannot find each other in the maze! Finally all are gathered to toast the couple.

---

3 Writing tips

There are many excellent books avail-able on developing writing skills, as well as courses and workshops. As a brief guide, aim to progress as follows:

1 Analyse the needs and strengths of the group.

2 Bearing this in mind, analyse the type and aims of the production.

3 Create a brief outline of the con-cept for approval.

4 Make a more detailed break-down of the plot. Show what happens within each scene.

5 Analyse the number of words that will be needed. Look at an existing play of suitable length; do a sample word count on a typical scene. Use this as a guide.

6 Write the play. Very roughly, some 10,000 to 12,000 words will pro-vide a sound script for the entire play. This count includes all the stage directions within the plot but excludes extraneous matter such as the list of characters, lighting plot and so on. Allow for intervals, music, and audience response.

Err on the short side rather than run-ning too long.

7 Take the provisional script along for the group or producer to read and discuss. Make any changes before creating final copies.

Approaching a new production

Approaching a new production

Rationalising aims

The committee or producer will need to plan ahead for each new production. Once the script is chosen or commissioned, the specific aims and needs of this particular show should be analysed and noted down as a basis for further planning – and then referred back to regularly throughout the production period.

An overall view

1

What is the type and style of the show?
(serious, comedy, revue and so on)

2

Why has the company chosen this vehicle?

3

What does everyone hope to achieve?

4

What sort of audience do you aim to attract – size, age group, intellect and so on

5

What particular problems, if any, does the production present? How do you aim to solve these?

6

How many are needed in the cast and backstage?

7

Are any unusual skills (or extra helpers) required?

8

What time span is needed for rehearsal?

Budget and finances

Planning a budget is discussed on pages 26 and 29. However, some feeling of what is available to spend and the financial commitment of the society to this particular production must be assessed at the same time as choosing a script. It is part and parcel of the choice. However, bear in mind that sometimes plays which cost more to present may make more money than small low-cost productions – provided that . . .

. . . the audience appeal is high

. . . a large cast (especially one involving children) is encouraged to attract greater audiences.

Whatever the play, someone who is good with figures and accountancy and able to control and oversee the spending, needs to be allocated the responsibility of doing this before the production is underway. They should simultaneously be given the appropriate information on funds available and intended spending.

Grants, subsidies and funding awards

It can be useful to appoint someone to investigate if any grants are available to the society. Local authorities, arts councils, regional art associations, and youth movements may be able to help. Lottery money can also be tapped for specific projects but all this takes considerable time and energy to organise. Ideally, a dedicated pertson or sub-committee should deal with all the paperwork and pitfalls.

The advice of someone who has already successfully gained a similar grant can be very useful and save much time (see also page 13).

The call-up

Front of stage

As soon as the play is chosen, contact all the existing active members. While this may be done initially by letter, a follow-up telephone call is always a good idea. It is much easier to convey excitement and tailor the 'call-up' specifically to the person to whom you are talking when you are conversing directly.

Make the recipient feel that this is a production not to be missed and that their particular contribution will be important.

Always:

Enthuse

Be positive

Director's check list

Name	'phoned	response
Mary R	✓	yes
David E	✓	?
Alice	✓	yes
Mary G	✓	no
Peter	✓	yes
George	✓	?
Gavin	✓	yes
Jaye		
Vivienne	✓	yes
Chris		
Barry		
Roger	✓	no
Norma	✓	yes
Marian	✓	yes

If yet more actors are needed, it may be worth:

1
Contacting other groups

2
Recruiting other new members from friends, colleagues, and existing actors' families. Bear in mind that untried actors often need a lot of help so do not tip the balance too far in this direction

3
Advertising: this can be a mixed blessing and may attract the very person you were hoping to avoid! However, provided there is a screening mechanism that allows you to reject applicants, there may be some useful gains. Never put 'Everyone welcome' unless this is countered by some such phrase as, 'in one capacity or another'!

4
Contacting past members

Backstage

It is vital to match abilities and attitudes to the particular demands of the jobs backstage, just as it is for front stage roles.

Obviously, some of these roles can be doubled up. For example, sound, lighting and special effects might come under a single person's jurisdiction. The set construction and painting hands often turn into stage hands for the production.

Generally about fifteen backstage and front of house personnel are required if no one person is to be overloaded. A lot depends on the intricacy and scale of the production, the number of scene changes, size of audience and so on.

Responsibilities and delegation

It is very important with any organisation for no one person to be overloaded. Apart from the fact that over-tiredness can take its toll, some abandoned families may begin to protest hotly if their husbands or mothers are never at home!

As well as directing the actors, in many local groups the producer is responsible for the backstage team too. There are many different ways to organise a show. Producers, while overseeing everything, will want greater input in certain areas than others – depending on which aspects of the production interest them most and on the demands of each particular play.

As a general rule, the producer or director will be responsible overall for the running of the production up until the first performance – when the Stage Manager takes charge. The charts on page 50 show this clearly.

To create a successful theatre company, it is important to create solid teams both on and off stage and to make sure no one person is overloaded beyond his or her capabilities.

You will need to find suitable people to undertake the following jobs:

Director and/or Producer
Actors
Stage manager
Stage hands
Wardrobe
Properties
Set designer
Set construction and painting
Lighting and Electrics
Sound
Special Effects
Make-up
Prompt
Publicity
Secretary

Creating tickets, posters and programmes
Keeping accounts
Selling tickets
Front of House

If required
Scriptwriter
Box Office
Catering
Waitresses
Bar Staff
Choreographer
Musicians
Pianist/Accompanist
Fundraisers

Organisation and 'red tape'

Whatever the size and 'formality' of the society, some organisation must be set in place to deal with the day-to-day running of the group. This might be a full committee with an official constitution, and an appointed chairman, secretary, treasurer and other officers. It might just be a hard-working but informal group who share the various duties. This will differ from one group to another but whatever the structure, there will be a great deal to organise and clear allocation of responsibilities is vital.

Certainly a secretary will be necessary to write and despatch all the letters, applications and notifications. The accounts must be kept in order and a mechanism for selling tickets established.

Most of the initial red tape will be dealt with by the secretary, but some delegation may be required if he or she is not to be overloaded.

The formalities

Putting on a show for public performance involves many layers of organisation. The audience welfare has to be considered so, in addition to all the organisation that the play itself requires, there will be numerous 'nitty-gritty' details to sort regarding insurance, safety and public health. All these formalities should be dealt with as soon as possible so that if there are any queries or hiccups, there is ample time to attend to these.

Some of the 'red tape' will be pertinent to the particular venue and will be the province of the local hall committee or whatever, but it is still the theatre company's responsibility to check that everything is in order. There is nothing worse than having to post-pone or cancel a play because the fire officer insists on new seating being installed or because you suddenly discover that the entertainment licence is not in place.

In an established society there is usually a committee or some system to deal with all the official 'red tape' but, for a newly formed group, these procedures will need to be investigated and set into action. All groups need to deal with the formalities well in advance of the performance.

Essential 'red tape'

Booking the hall

This is the kind of thing that everybody thinks someone else has done. Make sure that not only the dates of the performances are booked but that any essential rehearsal and set-erection time is also organised. You will also need sufficient time to clear up afterwards. A party after the Saturday performance will be short-lived if the hall has to be back to normal by 9 am the following morning for the local gym club – and might not happen at all if the booking expires on the same night. So reserve the dates required as soon as you know them. A well-organised society might book all the dates for an entire season's run of productions in one go.

Entertainment licence

Performing for a paying audience requires an entertainment licence. If the venue concerned has already been used for a production, by the local school, for example, then the licence may already exist but do ask and find out if this is indeed the case. It may have been ignored or not renewed! If the licence exists, check if it covers the dates you need. Also ensure that any specific requirements can be met, such as the correct proportion of toilets for the audience numbers expected. Otherwise your ticket sales may be restricted

There will, in any case, be a limit on audience capacity according to the size of hall concerned.

A seating plan will probably need to be submitted to the local authorities. Aisles need to be a particular width and exit signs clearly visible, with emergency batteries to keep them lit if there is a power failure. These should be standard fittings in a well used hall but make sure they are all in working order.

Insurance and public liability

In a public hall, insurance and public liability should be covered already. Once again, check that the policies are up to date and provide sufficient cover for both the audience and the group – for the rehearsal period and for performances.

Fire regulations

As in any situation when there are large numbers of people gathered together, the fire regulations can be quite strict. Fire officers are empowered to stop a show mid-performance if they feel the necessary precautions have not been taken. So it is important to make sure you are fully aware of the requirements.

Make sure that there are sufficient fire extinguishers, hydrants or hoses in good working order.

All the scenery must be fireproofed, including tabs and drapes. Buy fire-proofing crystals or sprays – or make up a mixture as follows:

15 ounces (425 gm) of boracic acid crystals
+
10 ounces (283 grams) of sodium phosphate
in
a gallon (4 litres) of water.

Check delicate fabrics first to see if there are any problems with colours running or shrinkage.

The company is obliged to inform the authorities of performance dates. Generally, fire prevention officers will call around prior to the show to check the venue. They will advise on any specific requirements. They will not be happy if flammable material is stored under the stage, for example, or if an exit is blocked, or if a fire escape is in an unsafe condition.

Sadly, real candles, for all their atmospheric flickering and shadows, will not be permitted. Find out about electric equivalents.

Pyrotechnics will have to comply with safety regulations too and must be operated by trained personnel. Special effects rental companies and the pyrotechnic operators can advise on this. The fire and/or police departments may need to be contacted for permission.

You may need a special licence to use a gun – even a starting pistol.

Electricity

It is vital to ensure that the electrical current supply is adequate to deal with all the lighting equipment that will be used. A vast battery of lights and special effects may stretch the theatre resources beyond the levels of safety. In the UK, the Electricity Board may provide an additional supply if necessary – and if given sufficient notice. In the USA, contact the Electrical Control Board with any queries.

Food and drink: health regulations and licences

Food

Current legislation imposes a fairly strict regime on the preparation of food for public consumption. If you wish to serve food in the intervals, it may prove simplest to stick to cold offerings and to prepare everything at home first.

Alcohol

Alcohol can be sold only under licence to adults. A member of the group will need to go to court to obtain this licence, and only so many licences will be available each year to any one group. In the UK, a local publican might provide a 'casual' licence. In either case, considerable notice is required. Set the wheels rolling as soon as the dates are fixed.

Copyright: scripts and music

Scripts

All published plays are protected by the copyright laws. Licences for performance and the costs of specific plays can be obtained by contacting the publishers.

Very occasionally, in special circumstances, when no charge is being made for admission and the performance is private – with the public excluded, performance fees may be minimal or waived altogether – but this is at the publisher's discretion and must be discussed with them; rights to perform the play will still need to be officially cleared.

A performance for charity is not excluded from paying fees. Copyright fees and royalties are still due to the authors, who depend upon these for their livelihood!

All clearance must be organised with the publishers prior to the performance. Normally fees are in proportion to the size of the venue and audience capacity so the small group pays far less than the large professional theatre. Regular users of a particular publisher's list may find it more convenient to open an account with the publishers to simplify payment and ordering of books.

Music

Music is protected in the same way. Sometimes a score may require a separate fee and license from the script. Check the small print!

If the music is not an integral part of the play, and has been selected from various other sources rather than being written specifically for the show, individual licenses for performance for each song will need to be obtained.

These are available in the UK from: The Performing Rights Society Limited, and in the USA from: ASCAP, BMI and SESAC.

See *Useful Addresses* on page 153-4.

The use of recorded music will also need to be cleared.

Video

To video a performance of a play usually needs its own specific copyright clearance.

An organised production

Task	Who is doing this	Date applied for	Date received
1 Book venue for performances			
2 Book venues for rehearsals			
3 Entertainment licence			
4 Submit seating plans			
5 Organise scripts or order play copies			
6 Sort license to perform play and pay royalties for this			
7 Check if a video is permissible; clear copyright for this			
8 Clear copyright for music and recordings			
9 Check insurance cover			
10 Check public liability			
11 Inform fire authorities			
12 Sort electrics			
13 Check health regulations if catering			
14 Organise licence to sell alcohol			

An organised production

Planning well and thinking ahead will make for a happier show.

The aim is to be efficient but adaptable when circumstances demand! A well organised production can cope with problems: a disorganised rabble may well founder!

The Budget

Every production – from the professional show to the village concert – requires some financing or backing. Money changes hands, even if only for programmes or coffees in the interval. Some ideas for fund-raising are discussed on page 13. It is very important to organise the finances properly and to keep clear records of

This form is free from copyright restrictions and so can be used for your own production (see page 147 for scaling information).

predicted and actual expenditure for future reference. Such records will be invaluable in estimating the costs of future productions.

An established society will have a savings or bank account holding the

Costs of each production

1
Red tape: licenses, insurance, copyright clearance and so on

2
Scripts and music scores

3
Schedules etc.: typing and photocopies

4
Hire of hall and rehearsal rooms

5
Costumes: making and hire

6
Makeup and wigs: restocking and hire, tissues and cold cream

7
Making the sets: materials, wood, canvas, fabric, paint, nuts and bolts and so on

8
Hiring set items

9
Lighting and electrics

10
Sound

11
Special effects

12
Properties

13
Any prizes or hand-outs to the audience

14
Publicity: posters, press advertisements, direct mail and any sundry advance information

15
Printing: tickets and programmes

16
Communications and administration: stamps and telephone calls

17
Catering: food, wine, coffees or whatever

18
Raffle prizes and tickets

19
Miscellaneous production costs, specific to the play

20
After-play parties and entertainment

21
Flowers (or equivalent) for the after-play presentations

22
Contingency allowance

Society expenditure and investment

This refers to long-term schemes for the society as a whole and covers those items which may not fall directly within the budget of the individual play, such as building a stage extension, repairs, new wings or steps, buying a carpet or a first-aid kit, cleaning/fire-proofing curtains, installing an intercom system, purchase of lighting equipment and so on.

Quite a number of these items, such as raffle prizes, typing, parties and telephone calls, may be offered free by members but they should still be listed and taken into account in case in future years this particular contribution is not forthcoming and must be funded from the budget.

More than one meeting will almost certainly be required to 'keep track' of production expenditure and to reassess the situation as it progresses in case cuts, fund-raising, the tightening (or loosening) of the purse-strings becomes appropriate.

It is also very useful to have a post-production meeting when all the bills have been amassed and paid. The society can then evaluate the success or otherwise of the production from a monetary point of view.

Pre-planning the production

Planning the technical aspects

The producer must have a feel for how the play will look and work before the production is underway. It will be essential to be familiar with the basic set design, entrances and exits before he or she can think clearly about the play and plot the moves. So it is important to meet the technical team as

profits from past productions which may suffice to finance the initial costs of the production. In due course, the money from advance sales of tickets will continue this process. However, it is still, of course, essential to impose certain limits on expenditure. While many productions will be self-supporting, profits can all too soon be squandered by an over-enthusiastic wardrobe or lighting department if given an 'open cheque book'!

Also, decisions have to be taken over the prices to be charged to the general public and, in general, how to balance the incoming revenue against the outgoing costs incurred.

Draw up an agenda for a budget meeting and discuss the costs with all concerned.

An organised production

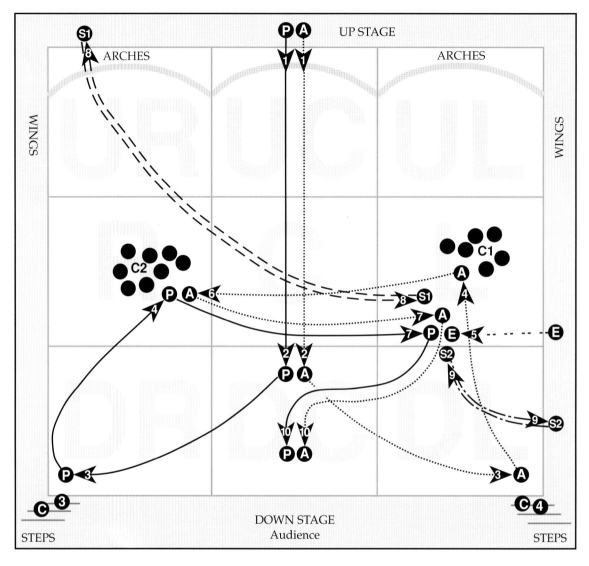

Key

A   Andrew
E   Edward
P   Pamela
S1 Servant
S2 Servant - Butler
C1 Crowd of villagers
    (Lynn & Kelly, David & Gill,
    Paul & Jenny)
C2 Crowd of villagers
    (Miles & Clare, Mark & Sian,
    Jim & Sue, Tony & Tessa)
C3 Children
    (Bob & Julie) ON STEPS DR
C4 Children
    (Patrick & Viv) ON STEPS DL

Moves

Villagers in pairs, men behind
women, arms around
waists, laughing, talking
1   P & A enter UC -
    Villagers cheer
2   P & A move DC

3   P & A separate
    A to C4, P to C3 -
    shake hands, kiss etc.
4   A to C1, P to C2 - mingle
5   E enters
6   A goes to P
7   A & P to E -
    shake his hand
8   S1 enters R with letter
9   A & P pass letter to S2
    who exits with it DL
10 A & P back to DC

early as possible to discuss ideas and to discover if specific pieces of equipment or recordings have to be ordered or made in advance. The full organisation of the technical aspects is covered in *Technical Teams* on pages 52-8 so, for now, all that needs to be said is that the earlier the team meet up, talk and share ideas, the better.

Plotting moves

Even before the play is cast, it can be very useful to plan the moves. This helps to develop the producer's vision of the play. Moreover, once rehearsals start, chaos will reign if no preparatory work has been done, especially when large numbers of people have to be manoeuvred around.

The moves should not be 'cast in stone': it is essential to keep an open mind during rehearsals so that moves remain reasonably fluid and can be adapted once the actors are on the stage. It is bound to look different and the actors' own instincts will develop the moves in different ways. The main aim is to be seen to be in control, to maximise rehearsal time and have a clear picture in your mind of the basic patterns being made – in particular entrances and exits and very busy scenes. The flow of movement should be smooth; it should avoid crowding, crossing and collisions.

Make a scale drawing of the stage floor plan. Then indicate the positions of furniture or props and entrances.

Characters, represented by coloured pieces of paper, chess pieces or the like can be moved around to enable some first decisions to be made.

Once you have created a satisfactory pattern of movement, superimpose these moves onto plans of the stage as lines with arrows. Use a different coloured pen for each character and then mark any stationary positions with a circle.

Photography and video

It is all too easy to overlook this element in the planning. However, since photography provides a great memento of each play, will help publicity and will create the backbone of

The New Players 1999 Rumpelstiltskin Budget		
Refreshments	£600.00	$900.00
Cotumes/wigs	£350.00	$525.00
Lighting	£400.00	$600.00
Hall hire	£450.00	$675.00
Scripts	£60.00	$90.00
License	£16.00	$24.00
Printing	£150.00	$225.00
Make-up	£50.00	$75.00
Sets + props	£300.00	$450.00
Flowers and gifts	£30.00	$45.00
Front of house	£20.00	$30.00
Total	**£2,426.00**	**$3,639.00**

Sensible planning of all the techniques and play requirements – whether sets or photography – can take place only when a budget has been established (see also pages 26-70). Here are a budget sheet and profit and loss report for a relatively low cost production

The New Players Rumpelstiltskin Christmas production 1999 Profit and loss report				
Income				
Ticket sales	£2,396.00		$3,594.00	
Bar takings	£907.39		$1,361.09	
Raffle	£151.50	**£3,454.89**	$227.25	**$5,182.34**
Costs				
Refreshments	£651.57		$977.36	
Cotumes/wigs	£300.77		$451.16	
Lighting	£400.00		$600.00	
Hall hire	£490.00		$735.00	
Scripts	£58.45		$87.68	
License	£10.00		$15.00	
Printing	Free		Free	
Make-up	£11.45		$17.18	
Sets + props	£213.35		$320.03	
Flowers and gifts	£32.00		$48.00	
Front of house	£19.81	**£2,187.4**	$29.72	**$3,281.13**
Profit		**£1,267.49**		**$1,901.21**

An organised production

the society's archive, it should be part of the pre-production organisation. More than one person may be needed, especially if you require both still photographs and a video.

Portraits of the cast help to boost interest in the forthcoming production

Try to set up the following:

1
Close-up photographs (portraits) of the cast for advertising the production as a display in local shops and as an 'appetiser' in the theatre foyer. You may already have portrait shots of existing members but will usually need to organise photographs of any new recruits. It is a good idea to take shots of the backstage team too. These photographs might also be used in the programme – and should certainly be included in the theatre archive

2
A 'formal' photograph of the entire cast and backstage team for each production

3
Press photographs of some of the cast as soon as the costumes are available

4
Photographs of rehearsals

5
Photographs of the play in performance

6
Some backstage candid shots!

7
A video of the performance. Several performances may need to be recorded and then edited together to ensure full coverage of the best moments

Members may require copies of the video so take orders for these beforehand – with cash 'up front'.

Establish an order mechanism for the still shots of the performance (see page 144). You will also need a clear account of who has paid!

The address book

Every society should set up its own address book. This will be invaluable in organising productions.

Collect together:

Names

Addresses with post codes

Telephone numbers (home and work for members of the group if possible)

Fax numbers

E-mail addresses

Include:

Active members

1
Producers and assistants

2
Acting members

3
Backstage team

4
Front of House helpers

5
Catering helpers

6
Photographers and video experts

Suppliers

1
Costume and wig hire

2
Lighting sales and hire

3
Sound equipment sales and hire

4
Set and property hire

5
Timber merchants

6
Paint suppliers

7
DIY shops

8
Professional caterers

9
Make-up suppliers

10
Electrical suppliers

11
Printers

12
Graphic designers

13
Wine merchants and glass hire companies

14
Wholesale food suppliers

15
Party suppliers

16
Curtain and fabric sources

17
Pyrotechnics suppliers and personnel

Publicity

1
Local press

2
Radio stations

3
Television stations

4
Local newsletter publishers

5
Drama news publishers

6
Libraries

7
Schools and colleges

8
Inns, pubs and restaurants

9
Shops

10
Any companies who advertise in the programme

11
Charity organisations

Society supporters

1
Patrons

2
Sponsors

3
Regular audience members

Red tape contacts

1
Hall committee contacts

2
Caretakers/janitors

3
Script sources and publishers

4
Performing Rights

5
Issuers of entertainment licences

6
Issuers of alcohol licences

7
Fire and safety officers

8
Electricity Board

9
Insurance contacts

10
Local council

11
Advisory groups

Other

1
Taxis and mini-buses

2
Other local groups and theatres

All systems go!

Now a good deal of the ground work has been done. With the project well planned, the 'red tape' dispensed with – or in hand – and organisation proce- dures set in place, it is time to begin in earnest and call up the acting mem- bers to audition. After all this excellent preparation, the production can be approached with confidence. Enthusiasm will be running high and the show will be launched in an air of optimism and exhilaration – the best possible start of all.

Auditions and casting

Auditions can be exhilarating and exciting but are never easy. The elements of competition and of being 'on trial', just like any examination or test, can be stressful for the actors taking part and impose great responsibilities on those in the seat of judgement. It is essential to try to be fair – and to be seen to be so. To always try to help everyone to relax so that they can do their best, and to create an air of confidence by working within a well-planned structure.

Key points to a good audition

Pre-plan well

The more ground work that is put in before everyone gathers together, the more smoothly the auditions will go. This is vital. A muddled audition will diminish confidence in the proceedings. Also, for most of the actors this will be their first exposure to the play – and first impressions count for a lot. The producer must know the script inside out, have planned the auditions thoroughly, ooze enthusiasm and be in control.

A good turn-out

There is nothing more disappointing than waiting all night in an empty hall for your potential cast to arrive. Your excitement about the show will soon vanish if only one or two members turn up to audition. So the first essential is to make sure all members of the society are informed and suitably enthused.

In a large society, where parts are at a premium, there may be a huge list of available actors, many more than the play demands. In this situation, the telephone calls may not be necessary or economical but there may still be

---

Plan of campaign to ensure a full audition

1
Book the audition dates at the venue

2
Analyse the play

3
Select audition sections, if appropriate

4
Send out :

– notification of auditions
– a résumé of the play
– audition pieces, if required
– a 'response mechanism' (for example a 'tear-off' form or a request that each actor telephones you) so that recipients contact you to confirm their interest

5
Telephone to chat about the play and to remind the actors of the audition dates, especially to those who have not responded via the return mechanism

---

certain eminently suitable 'targets' that you wish to ensure come along.

A balanced and informed approach

There is an element, of course, in every casting, of the director having some preconceived ideas about who will play what. The most important thing is to keep these premature notions in line. Be open-minded, allow yourself see other possibilities and try to discover the cast's feelings about particular roles. If Simon is longing to

---

be a villain, at least ensure that he has the chance to audition for one. And if the last thing in the world that Jane wants to do is to be yet another bland heroine, then give her a meaty role to try in the auditions.

The audition form

Ask the actors to fill in a form about the kind of part they want to play This can be circulated during the reading or audition. It will serve as a handy memory-jogger later, as well as an invaluable list of telephone numbers. Ask for information about the particular roles the actors would like to try as well as general comments on the type and size of roles that appeal and whether or not they are willing to help back-stage, too.

It can be very useful to find out the heights of the actors at this stage – an invaluable piece of information later if pairing up couples for chorus work, working out crowd scenes or organising line-ups with the taller actors at the back.

Discover the actors' reactions

Not everyone expresses their real feelings on a publicly shared document. With a 'stock company', there is nothing like relaxed conversation to draw out the truth! Meeting up for a drink or coffee after the first audition will allow a more open expression of views. It can be useful, anyway, to hear everyone's ideas about the play and you may be able to tease out some genuine reactions to the role options.

It is impossible to please everyone, of course. You cannot cast six people in a single leading role but knowing what people would really like to do is a very useful guide – and can hold quite a few surprises.

Starlight Players

Starlight Players are now planning their September production:

Falling Leaves: a cabaret

Please come to one or more of the auditions on
Wednesday 21 May
Thursday 22 May
or Monday 26 May

This should be a very exciting and lively production with plenty of chances for everyone to be involved. There will be music, dance, comic sketches, lots of singing, magic, and a few speciality acts – we plan to include a comic fire-eating act and a silent movie routine.
So there will lots of fun and lots of hard work. We should be glad of your support.

Please complete the form below and return by 17 May to
John Craft
The Cottage
Slipton
Halltown West

We should be delighted if any backstage members would like to attend, too. It is a great opportunity to meet up and to find out early what the production will involve.

While precedence will be given to those actors who turn up, if you cannot attend on any of these dates, but would like to be involved, front or backstage, please telephone John Craft (1637 9999) or Gill Payne (2279 0123) to discuss.

Please let us know if there is anyone new you think we should contact this time . . .

Meanwhile, we look forward to seeing you soon.

Best wishes　　　*Gill X*　　　Gill Payne

Name　　　　　　　　　　　　　　　　Telephone
Address　　　　　　　　　　　　　　　Fax
　　　　　　　　　　　　　　　　　　E-mail

Please tick the appropriate boxes

☐ I would like to be considered for a part in **Falling Leaves**　☐ Sorry, I cannot be involved this time

I shall be coming to the audition(s) on
☐ Wednesday 21 May　☐ Wednesday 21 May　☐ Thursday 22 May　☐ Monday 26 May

☐ I would prefer to help backstage

I am especially interested in a　☐ singing part　☐ dancing part　☐ acting part　☐ comic part

Key points to a good audition

Audition form	Play *Murder with Music*		Date *20 November*
Name	Gill Brooklyn	Susan Holder	Geoff Taylor
Name for programme	Gillian Brooklyn	ditto	ditto
Address	The Trees	12 Peach Road	3 Field Road
	23 Green Lane	Uppington Village	Cranog Village
	Pinktown	near Vantage	near Vantage
Post code/Zip	WA12 3AS	UA34 3DS	UA34 2SD
Telephone home	01234 56789	04321 56789	04321 98765
Telephone work	01732 90631		Please do not 'phone
Fax home	01234 56788		me at work
Fax work	01732 90629		
E-mail	g.brooklyn@text.com	s.holder@text.com	g.taylor@text.com
Mobile telephone	0777 98765	0777 23456	0777 12345
Height	5 feet 7ins	5 feet 4ins	6 feet 1ins
Role preferred	Sally	Mrs Lambert	Will do anything
comments	Lots of lines but I am sure I can cope	Don't want a big part	
Will you sing?	Yes but not solo	Only if forced	Yes
Will you dance?	Yes	No	Yes
Back stage		Yes	Yes
which capacity		Costumes	Sets
skills		Sewing/hemming	Carpentry
Other	Wednesdays are difficult	Would like to act with	
i.e. Is there a night you cannot come to rehearsals?	but not impossible	Jenny again	

This form is an invaluable record of who attended the auditions and their reactions to the script.

It is useful to know heights when planning chorus work, line-ups and how to pair couples sensibly.

The form is a sound basis for updating name, address and telephone listings.

It also helps you to check name spellings for the programme – and to find out if someone prefers to have a different name in the programme.

They may have a stage name or prefer to use an unmarried name - or simply the formal name rather than a familiar one!

Team building

A good audition will help ascertain just who is the best actor for each part but there are other factors to take into account before finally casting. The most important aim is that, once the production is underway, the cast must gel as a team. How people work together is very important – so choose the right person for the part, taking the overall picture into consideration. Finding the appropriate blend of personalities, choosing reliable hard-working people who learn their lines, and endeavouring to give a fair distribution of roles over the years can contribute more to a good, happy production than simply picking the most obvious talent.

Action plan for the auditions

The auditions can take several forms. Generally they fall into the following patterns:

1
A read-through of the script, with the actors sitting down

2
A read-through of pre-selected excerpts, with the actors sitting down

3
An enactment on the stage of pre-selected excerpts, with the actors moving

4
Set audition pieces – that actors may or may not have been given beforehand. These will be performed on the stage

5
A combination of the above

Types of audition and structure

Order of events

Whether the audition is a simple read-through or a reading of selected pieces, the following order applies:

1 Give a pep talk: explain the major points of the play, the society's reasons for doing this production and any personal enthusiasms. Discuss aims, roles and the most exciting aspects of the production. Inspire everyone!

2 Pass around the audition form to be completed. Make sure everybody fills this in by the end of the evening.

3 Read the play or a selection of excerpts.

4 Ask actors to perform audition pieces, if these are being included.

5 Sum up again the play's exciting possibilities; include any thoughts the audition has inspired.

6 Thank everyone for coming.

7 Progress somewhere informal to talk.

Sometimes actors may ask if they can take their play copies away with them. If another audition is planned and there are only a few reading copies, these may need to be retained.

If, on the other hand, there are sufficient copies available and the actor is a serious contender for a role, it may help him or her to gain a better understanding of the play by reading the script again – especially if there are no other gatherings planned before the first rehearsal.

If you do decide to part with any scripts, first ascertain that the actor is definitely willing to take part, and that he or she agrees to be responsible for returning the copy if there is any problem later. Then, most important of all, write down the actor's name in a 'Copies given out' list – straight away, before you forget who has taken them away!

Read-throughs

Ideally, a first read-through should not act as the 'real' audition but as a means of allowing the group – in particular, the potential members of the cast and back-stage team – to become familiar with the play. As a bonus, hearing the play being read aloud helps the producer to evaluate its strengths and weaknesses, how long it is, whether cuts are required and which are the most humorous or dramatic moments.

In practice, the first read-through will often feel like an audition and, because of the pressure of time, is taken as such. However, a second read-through will generally prove a better testing point for the actors' abilities and suitabilities.

Try to sit in a circle. Directors should sit in a position where they can see everyone and be aware of late arrivals, and who has not yet read. There is nothing worse for an actor than turning up to audition and then sitting in silence all evening.

Audition pieces

For a 'stand-up' audition, pick out those scenes that best test the ability of the actors to interpret the characters concerned. Try to strike a balance between those scenes demanding flamboyant acting and 'quieter' ones.

Audition hazards

This will enable you to assess the actors when they are performing in a controlled and disciplined way, as well as when they are giving full vent to dramatic energy.

Copies of one or two pertinent extracts can be handed out beforehand so that contenders can 'mug them up'. During the audition, these sections of script can be repeated several times with different groups of people acting.

It will be important to analyse how the different actors interact. Casting decisions will, in part, depend on both the physical relationship and the 'chemistry' of the pairs and groups of actors who will share the stage. Make sure the selected scenes allow these relationships to be explored in full.

Audition hazards

Pre-casting

1 Do not decide in advance who should play which role. Let the possibilities flow.

2 As best you are able, within the limits of time and impossible casting, give everyone a chance to audition for the roles they would like to play.

3 Do not fall into the trap of type-casting. Always attempt to stretch the actors by trying them out in different kinds of role.

Newcomers

1 Do not treat new members as outsiders or they may never be seen again. Make every one who turns up to the auditions feel as welcome as possible, with ample opportunity to read or perform.

2 Because new members are untried material, they will need special attention. To some degree, the directors already understand the abilities of well-tried players. The performance in audition of new members should be assessed with particular care.

3 Although new members may have had experience elsewhere, it can be dangerous to give them major roles before discovering their limitations. Some actors who audition brilliantly cannot learn lines or never turn up to rehearse. These characteristics are impossible to detect in an audition. So be relatively cautious in your casting.

No shows!

Every society has these – the actors who believe that their talents are such that they do not actually need to audition. To be fair to everyone else, try to ensure that all prospective actors, however talented, turn up for at least one audition.

Concentration problems

1 Do not tell actors too far in advance that they are to read a particular role. They will immediately thumb ahead through the script and start practising mentally, oblivious to the rest of the play being read. When their turn does arise, they will have lost their place.

2 Look and listen. In a read-through, do not concentrate on voices only. Try to observe expressions and instinctive gestures as well.

Casting factors

Consider the following:

Acting ability

Acting ability is obviously a major consideration. Carefully chosen audition pieces should allow abilities to be evaluated and compared. It is always interesting how differently individual actors approach a role so keep an open mind over interpretation.

Bear in mind some of those auditioning may be very nervous and will perform far better when cast and in rehearsal than in auditions – also that some superb acting talent can be concealed by poor reading abilities.

Being nervous about mispronunciation or misinterpretation may disguise competent acting skills.

Physique

Does the actor have the appropriate visual appearance? Is he or she the right height, shape, size, colouring and age group for the part? And if not, how important is this? Could make-up and costume redress the balance? Does the stature or age need to complement any other actor's build or years?

Movement

Does the actor move well? Beginners often need guidance on what to do with their hands and find it difficult to keep still. Natural movement and gestures are a great asset.

Voice

1 Voice projection is important. Can the actor be heard? Audibility is absolutely vital.

2 Does the voice sound right for the character?

3 Does the voice complement other actors' voices who are sharing the stage? For example, two very similar voices can make the dialogue sound boring and monotonous.

4 Does the voice sound right for the age of the role? Although make-up and costume can create the illusion of youth or age, an inappropriate voice is often a complete give-away!

'Feelings'

Does the interpretation feel right? Does the actor seem comfortable with the role? Is this a part they will relish playing – or take up as a challenge? Try to determine the actor's attitude and level of enthusiasm.

Will the teams and pairs gel?

All these factors – acting technique, stance, stature, voice and suitability for the part must work in relationship to the others on the stage.

1 If a pair are total extremes in height, for example, this could work very well for a comedy duo but would not suit a romantic couple.

2 The voices must sound right together, too.

3 Some groups of actors work especially well together. A good, well-bonded pair or group will energise each other and rehearse very happily together. Humour can be sparked off by a good comedy partnership and emotional scenes will work best if the actors react well to each other's 'chemistry'.

4 At the other end of the spectrum, personality clashes can wreak havoc in a production. Of course, two strong personalities with different ideas can be manipulated constructively, if their energy can be 'channelled' into a stimulating reaction between the two, but the director needs to be courageous and strong to handle this kind of scenario!

5 There are also practical considerations. If two of the actors are never available on the same evening, they will be for ever playing opposite 'stand-ins'.

Decision making

male and female roles into two columns and then do the same with the actors. Also make note of any roles that might be played by either sex (see also page 19), roles that might be split into two parts instead of one, and any ideal 'pairings' of actors.

It will probably take several experiments before you feel that you have the best possible casting. Then, inevitably, someone will telephone and say that he or she is being sent abroad and so is no longer available. If the actor was playing a major role, the entire casting may have to be rethought!

Announcing the cast

Some societies read out the casting at the next gathering. However, if it is possible, inform the players of your decisions by letter or telephone.

This is particularly important for those whom you know will be most grieved. Announcing the cast in front of all and sundry is uncomfortable for the disappointed. Some actors can feel very upset. And even those who have been given the parts find their pleasure curbed by their awareness of the others in their midst who have been less fortunate. Moreover, a personal conversation gives you time to discuss the role with the actor and prepare the ground for forthcoming rehearsals.

Once the casting is finalised, everyone can look forward to seeing the play take shape. Draw up a final cast list and distribute this to all the members of the team concerned. For example, the wardrobe department will need to know as soon as possible whom they are dressing and how!

Now the next stage is to stir the backstage team into action!

Decision making

It is time to make the decisions.

The complications depend upon the size of the cast and the numbers auditioning. If the play has approximately the same number of parts as potential cast then, although there may need to be a good deal of 'juggling about' to attain the best result, at least there will be fewer disappointed actors!

Keep those who are less experienced, new, or less competent in smaller or chorus roles so that they have the opportunity to learn and gain confidence, without the central core of the play suffering. While the society will want to be fair to all its members, if the group is to attract and maintain audiences, it is vital that the paying public are given their due, too. At the end of the day, every group's future depends on pleasing and retaining its audiences. It is not always easy to keep the balance just right!

To help the decision making, take careful notes during the auditions and read these thoroughly, together with the actors' comments on the audition form, before drawing up the first attempt at casting.

Casting sheet

Casting sheets help the brain to think! Write down the roles with plenty of space next to each for notes and names. If the cast is large, separate the

Casting sheet: **The Bride of Doom**

Main female roles 4   Main male roles 4   Others: minimum 3 children, 2 female, 2 male

Female roles: potential actresses

Janet Biggings	Tania Williams	Susan Sharp	Philippa Jones
Sue Colting	Hannah Richards	Gill Dash	Sheila Pick
Sarah Leighton	Jaquie Edwards		

	1st choice	2nd choice	3rd choice
Mrs Maple	Tania Williams	Sarah Leighton	
Isadora Maple	Hannah Richards	Phillppa Jones	
Jenny, the maid	Sue Colting	Jaquie Edwards	Gill Dash
Mrs Chesterman	Janet Biggings		

Male roles: Potential actors

| Tom Biggings | Phil McGregor | Tony Adams | John David |
| David Colting | Jack Colting | Philip Dash | |

	1st choice	2nd choice	3rd choice
Mr Maple	Tom Biggings	John David	David Colting
Lord Doom	Jack Colting	Tony Adams	
Jeremy Gardens	Phil McGregor		
John Hero	Philip Dash	Tony Adams	

Either/or roles:

Children
| Sally Colting | John Dash | Peter Henry | Simon Colting |
| Sophie O'Kelly | Belinda Kellerman | Jenny Pick | |

Villagers
| Susan Sharp | Sheila Pick | plus whoever when main roles cast | |

Wedding guests
| Susan Sharp | Sheila Pick | plus whoever when main roles cast | |

Creating the Support Team

Choosing the best possible technical back-up and support team is as important as choosing the best possible cast. The polish of the final production will depend upon the expertise behind the scenes and the relaxation of the audience will depend upon a smooth-running front-of-house organisation.

Just as with the audition decisions regarding the on-stage team, personalities and competence are as important as the knowledge and talent of the off-stage team.

The ability to work well with others, to delegate as necessary and to complete tasks in good time will be vital.

This chapter concentrates on who is needed for back-up and explains their ideal qualities as part of the team. More technical planning is discussed in *Technical Teams* on pages 52-8.

The backstage team

Finding help

Start early

It is wise to begin early with appointing the backstage staff. Do not assume that the usual people will be available or that it will be a simple matter to recruit help. The more time that is available, the easier it will be for each department to complete its tasks thoroughly and punctually and, in turn, to appoint its own team of helpers as required.

Sources of help

1 The hard-core team
Established societies generally build up a 'backbone' of members who are always willing to work behind the scenes. Indeed, a good number of these proclaim they would never wish to appear on stage. They enjoy the challenge of helping to create a play without the onus of line-learning and performing in public.

2 Acting members
Sometimes help may be recruited from acting members who have not been cast. The audition forms will have discovered which ones are willing to do this and, after the play, many comment how much they have enjoyed the experience.

It is also very useful for actors to discover what life is like behind the scenes. Often they have remained unaware of the hard work involved – and of the satisfaction that can be gained when the job is done well.

3 Family and friend recruits
Families and friends of the acting members can often be encouraged to lend a hand backstage, if there is a shortage of help.

Ideally, any new, raw recruits should be placed under the guidance of an established 'department head' until they have become familiar with the routine.

4 Other societies
Backstage staff from other local groups may be willing to help, especially if your society has a crisis, such as the lighting expert suddenly being taken ill.

5 Professional help
Professional skills can be hired. Stage magazines carry advertisements for these personnel. In the case of electrics, pyrotechnics, flying people and other such potentially dangerous pursuits, professional help will, in any case, be mandatory.

Who fits which slot?

The stage manager

> **The ideal stage manager is:**
>
> **1**
> Calm
>
> **2**
> Authoritative, and commanding of respect
>
> **3**
> Highly organised
>
> **4**
> Able to concentrate
>
> **5**
> A good communicator
>
> **6**
> Good at handling emergencies

The stage manager is the producer's right-hand person. A good, experienced and responsible stage manager will organise all the back-stage team and will be totally in charge of the running of the show during the performances, from opening the curtain on the first scene to deciding how many final bows the cast need to take in the finale.

Stage managers need to oversee all the set and property changes. Sometimes stage managers are involved in the construction of the sets. If not, they will need to become familiar with the function and requirements of the scenery, as well as the properties and special effects.

In addition, they should watch the latter rehearsals, taking close note of the director's aims, checking the curtain timing and writing down the major backstage demands.

The backstage team

The stage manager needs to exercise discipline and diplomacy so as to manage all the actors competently (the tense, stressed ones and the laid-back-*is-it-really-my-cue-now?* variety) and to make sure they are ready for their entrances.

The stage manager also has to oversee the entire backstage team and do his or her best to ensure a smooth-running technical performance every night, from the dress rehearsal onwards.

Stage hands

> **The ideal stage hand is:**
>
> **1**
> Relatively strong
>
> **2**
> Cheerful, with a sense of humour
>
> **3**
> Happy to take orders from the stage manager
>
> **4**
> Able to move quietly and quickly

Stage hands must be able to move scenery and large properties calmly, quickly and quietly. They should be aware of exactly when these moves are needed and the precise location of each piece. An awareness of the plot and the flow of the play will help to avoid any gross error such as setting the wrong scene. While a good stage manager should be checking on everything, the more people that understand exactly what is needed, and when, the less likely such a blunder becomes.

If they have to appear in front of the audience, stage hands are best either dressed simply in inconspicuous black or in a costume that is appropriate to the play – as footmen or servants, perhaps – whatever suits the theme.

Wardrobe

> **The ideal head of wardrobe is:**
>
> **1**
> A good tailor or seamstress with own sewing machine – who can work quickly
>
> **2**
> Artistic and creative
>
> **3**
> Imaginative
>
> **4**
> Able to locate relatively inexpensive sources of fabric or costumes
>
> **5**
> Well organised
>
> **6**
> Sensitive; able to appreciate the needs of the play and the players
>
> **7**
> Able to work within a budget

Most of the wardrobe's responsibilities are dealt with prior to the performance when either one person, or a whole team of people, will find, alter, hire or create the costumes required for the production.

It is useful, however, if a wardrobe person can be available backstage during the performances too – to help with difficult or fast changes and to have safety pins plus a needle threaded and ready for instant repairs.

A good wardrobe head will be able to create visual impact through colour and styling, design and flair – all of which should reflect the theme, style and feeling of the play, as well as any historical setting.

The producer and wardrobe need to discuss the play as early as possible. Ideas about characters and style, colour and fabric need to be established promptly so that the accumulation of materials can begin Once the characters have all been cast, measurements can be taken and work will begin in earnest.

Throughout rehearsals, the costume department will need to liaise closely with the producer so that they are aware of any changes or additional requirements.

Properties

> **Ideal Properties staff are:**
>
> **1**
> Good at making things – imaginative and creative
>
> **2**
> Confident and persuasive
>
> **3**
> Very well organised and good at organising others
>
> **4**
> Tidy; enjoy putting things in order
>
> **5**
> Happy to take responsibility

Property personnel need to be creative and imaginative in order to find, adapt or make properties. They also need to be utterly charming – so that they can coerce others into lending

41

The backstage team

the society furniture or whatever is needed. They need to be able to co-ordinate with the set designer over size, colour and shape of any large-scale props when these are an integral part of the overall scene.

As well as furnishings, the property department will be dealing with a multitude of smaller items – everything from china, books and clocks to strings of sausages.

Personal properties

Small personal props – for instance, watches, handkerchiefs, notebooks (anything worn or pocketed) will need to be sourced by Props. However, once handed over, these become the responsibility of the actor concerned until their safe return after the show. None the less, it will be useful if Props can double check everything, personal props included, as the show rolls.

The set designer

> **The ideal set designer is**
>
> **1**
> Artistic and imaginative
>
> **2**
> Able to communicate ideas well
>
> **3**
> Highly practical as well as artistic – the sets must work
>
> **4**
> Able to liaise well with the producer

Set design, like costumes, is a pre-production activity. It is vital to plan the set very early so that the producer can plot the play, understanding exactly how all the entrances and exits work.

Then, during rehearsals, the director can 'mock up' on stage entrances and important structures, chalk in sight-lines and so on.

The set designer needs to understand the play well and to interpret both the author's and the producer's concepts in a practical but exciting way.

From the dress rehearsal onwards, the set is really in the hands of the stage manager. Once watching out front, of course, the designer is likely to see elements that need improving and, if time allows, may be tempted to titi-vate before the opening night!

The good set designer is sympathetic to the mood and aspirations of the

show. The sets may create everything from a kitchen to a palace, a desert island to a snowscape, using form and colour, light and shadow, patterns and texture as well as physical structures.

The designer may or may not construct and paint the set. If this task falls to others, however, the designer must be able to delegate constructively, explain clearly what is needed and check regularly that the sets are turning out as he or she envisioned.

The images must retain their integrity and flow through the practical translation into timber, fabric, light and paint – and, ultimately, reach the audience in the way intended.

Lighting

The ideal lighting expert is

1
A good electrician

2
Aware of all the dangers and safety methods

3
Artistic and imaginative

4
Willing to experiment

5
Calm and organised

6
Familiar with the equipment: hopefully he or she, or the theatre company, will own some pieces

In professional theatre there is a clear distinction between those who design the lighting for plays and those who organise the electrics. In amateur theatre these distinctions blur and it is likely to be a single person (plus, perhaps, one or two helpers on the mechanical side) who works out the lighting plot, designs the colour and light effects, who clambers up ladders and scaffolding to rig the lights – and who then, finally, presses all the buttons and dimmer switches during the performances.

It is an artistic and highly technical role. However, most electricians – while they might be novices in the world of theatre – can, with enthusiasm, study of the specific techniques and/or the guidance of someone with experience, manage to light a show adequately, even with limited equipment. Combine this with a little flair, and the new lighting personnel can achieve really good results. It is vital to have a very clear understanding of electrical safety.

Obviously good equipment makes an enormous difference to what can be achieved, but if the lights are being hired, there will be little time to practise before the dress rehearsals.

If everything is well organised and thoroughly rehearsed beforehand, and time is allowed for at least one thorough, intensive technical rehearsal, then smooth progress should be ensured. Never choose a lighting person who is prone to panic!

Sound and special effects

All that has been said about lighting applies in a similar way to the sound and special effects personnel. They will need the same qualities – and to be equally practical and imaginative. If pyrotechnics are involved, professional advice and staff will be needed.

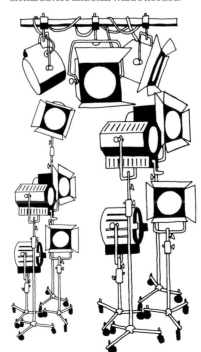

Make-up

The ideal make-up artist is:

1
Creative

2
Understands faces and the use of shadows and highlights

3
Calm – able to make the actors relax

4
Happy to experiment and research before the show

5
Well-organised

6
Good at delegating

In the right hands, make-up can add hugely to the success of the production. While experience or expertise are useful, enthusiasm and imagination are equally important – and the newcomer can learn a great deal under the tutelage of an expert or from the many excellent books available on the subject.

For a large cast, extra help may be needed, if only to put on foundation and base make-up, leaving the more complicated details to the more experienced make-up artists.

Certain actors prefer to do their own make-up and can become expert at this but it is still important that one person generally keeps an eye on the rest of the team's efforts and takes an overall view of the make-up to ensure that the production has a cohesive style and approach.

Other important help

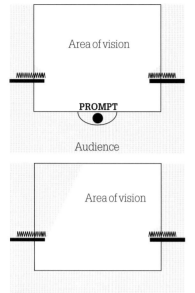

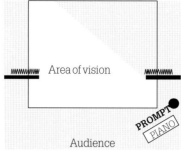

Other important help

The prompt

The ideal prompt . . .
1
Has a sense of humour

2
Is calm, collected and organised

3
Has a clear, audible voice

4
Can concentrate for long periods
and is not easily distracted

5
Enjoys the commitment

6
Can make decisions very quickly

A good prompt is vital – to producer
and cast alike. It is not always an easy

*It is important that prompts can see
and hear the actors clearly. A discreet
position is useful so that the audience
are not too aware of the presence of
the prompt. However, since it is most
important that the prompt can see the
actors' expressions, do not sacrifice
this element in order to hide prompts
away. Dress them in suitable
costume, if necessary!*

task and requires enormous concentration, with no breaks throughout the
performances and no real apprecia-
tion by the audience of services
rendered!

Some people love prompting, especially if they enjoy drama but do not
wish to be in the limelight themselves. However, there is little
opportunity to relax and the prompt
can become the target for abuse if the
dialogue goes awry! Moreover, poring
over small print can cause eye strain.
Make an enlarged duplication of the
script and provide good light in the
prompt's corner.

Producers must consistently update
the prompt with all the necessary
background information about the
play and players, any changes or
omissions to the script, vital pauses
and 'shaky' areas. Early attendance at
rehearsals will enable the prompt to
get to know the play intimately. It will
then be easier to be a little more
relaxed during performances.

Prompt responsibilities

**To prompt and help during
rehearsals**
The prompt is an invaluable aid to
line-learning and should attend
rehearsals at least as soon as the
first actors put down scripts. The
prompt can help keep track of the
script during rehearsals, mark up
cues and note practical points, as
well as prompting – so that the
producer can concentrate on
watching what is happening
on stage.

**To prompt well during
performances**
Prompts must speak up quickly
whenever actors lose their lines
and so keep the show rolling. To do
this well, the prompt must :

1
Know the play inside out

2
Understand the individual actors'
interpretation, timing and attitude

3
Be aware of each actor's line-
learning abilities, and which
sections of dialogue have proved a
problem during rehearsals

4
Be able to be heard – and to
respond quickly. It is pointless for a
prompt to whisper if the actor
cannot hear the cue. Nothing is
more uncomfortable for an
audience than to watch an actor
struggling to find his words with no
sound from the prompt corner. A
clear, confident cue is always a
welcome relief

Other important help

The good prompt, who knows the play and actors intimately, will be aware of problems immediately and will give the line before the audience has noticed that there is a gap. Being able to see the stage and the actors' expressions is an enormous help: these can be a trigger to the prompt to respond. Prompts should be sensitive to the actor's reactions at all times so that they do not jump in unnecessarily every time an actor pauses for dramatic effect. Neither should they let an actor flounder around ad-libbing furiously, believing that the actor must be coping.

The prompt will need to mark up pauses, cuts, changes and any 'sticky' areas on the script

Prompts need to control the flow.

If actors suddenly jump forward or back in the script – or if a section of dialogue seems about to repeat itself, it is the responsibility of the prompt to guide the actors back to the correct place in the script. Should the actors not respond and seem to be continuing with the momentum of the new position in the play, the prompt, while not deserting his or her post, should relay a message to the stage manager – as the repercussions can be devastating to others involved. Actors may have to change costumes at lightning speed or alter lines to suit the new circumstances. Technicians may need to revise the flow of sound and light-

ing effects, caterers prepare the interval beverages at breakneck speed – and so on. Often, the audience will be totally oblivious to the chaos reigning backstage!

The prompt copy

In some theatres, the prompt acts as assistant to the stage manager and is responsible not only for prompting the actors but also for cueing the lighting, sound and special effects. Whatever the area of responsibilities, the prompt should make up a 'prompt copy'

Scale up the script to a achieve better legibility and then insert it into a folder, with loose leaves in between. This will allow ample space for notes on all the cues, front and backstage, and for marking in actors' dramatic pauses and potential stumbling points

1
Make sure both file and paper used are sturdy enough to take the continuous handling through rehearsals and performances

2
Do not underestimate the amount of information it will need to contain. Make sure there is room to accommodate all the rehearsal notes, back-stage cues, and last-minute changes

3
Keep it tidy and legible. This document will be an invaluable point of reference for the producer during rehearsals and later, for the stage manager in performances; it may well serve as the basis for the stage manager's 'bible'

Enter three young fellows, Cedric, Fred and Charles, in striped blazers and boaters.

Cedric Oh, I say, you fellows, just come and look at this view. . .

Fred Yes, the whole jolly sweep of Sundown Bay is simply spread out before us.

Charles I don't think Cedric's admiring the landscape. I think he's got his monocle trained on that spiffing view just down there.

Fred Oh . . . oh, you mean–
Keeps forgetting line!

Charles Yes, the girls!

Cedric The girls, the girls, my dear chap! Why do you think we've come here today? Look at 'em, just look at 'em!
Slight pause as they gaze out

Charles All those dinky little knees out for an airing in the sun!
Fred pauses here /

Fred Golly!/Well, my Mater always says that fresh air and exercise stimulate the appetite!

Cedric *(laughing)* Ha! Who needs stimulation, hey what? Wah, wah!

Charles Wah, wah, wah, wah!

Fred Wah, wah, wah– But I thought we'd come here for a little paddle, chaps ?

Cedric Well, that's a frightfully sporting idea, I must say. Let's go and test the jolly old waters, eh! But hang the paddle! I vote we go for the full immersion job. Hey what?

Fred But it's too bally cold!

Charles And it's too bally wet! Wah, wah!
Cedric cuts in

Cedric And it's too bally beautiful to resist! Just think of it, old sports, all those delicious darlings down there disporting in the waves, practically undressed. Just waiting for us.

Fred Oh gosh!

Cedric Look! Take a peek at that redhead in the clinging stripes.

Charles *(wolf-whistles)* What a spiffing little figure.
Pause as Cedric crosses stage

Cedric *(adjusting monocle)* Not so little, dear fellow. Those stripes are shooting all over the place. Corr!!

Fred Golly! My Mater's warned me about red-heads.
Pause

Cedric I say, do be careful, old chap! You're steaming up my monocle.

Other important help

Front of House

The staff at the front of house are the first people that the audience meet when they arrive so it is fundamental that they are cheerful and smiling, giving a warm welcome to all. Greet everyone who arrives. Make them feel good and relaxed.

Front of House responsibilities

In some societies, Front of House may simply involve selling tickets and programmes at the door. In others, the duties might begin with the organisation of the entire sale of tickets from their day of issue to the tidying up of the hall at the end of the run. Generally, the following needs to be accomplished:

**The ideal
Front of House staff are:**

1
Cheerful

2
Charming

3
Diplomatic

4
Unflustered

5
Smiling

6
Able to cope with emergencies

7
Able to handle money
responsibly

8
Conscious of audience safety
and comfort

The venue

**Make sure the venue is
organised. This might
include overseeing:**

1
Seating

2
Table arrangements and
tablecloths

3
Numbering seats

4
Audience entrances and exits

5
Photographs of show or cast

6
Flower arrangements

7
Music playing

Tickets

Sell tickets in house (and sometimes in advance). Collect cash or cheques, and account for any monies received.

(Publicity and ticket sales are discussed in more detail in *Publicity* on pages 104-119.)

Catering

Ensure the caterers have everything they need, that food and drink is ready on time and that waiters, waitresses or bar staff are all organised.

Usherettes and programme selling

Help the audience to find their places and offer each one a programme.

The Raffle

Organise the display of gifts, sale of raffle tickets, the draw and presentation of prizes.

Reservations

Deal with tickets held at the door and any reserved places.

Communication with backstage

Front of House may need to communicate with the Stage Manager as the main link with the backstage team. Their knowledge of the situation in the audience means they can say whether or not the play (or an act) should begin – or be held back – because of last-minute arrivals.

Latecomers

Deal with latecomers quietly and efficiently.

Say goodbye

See everyone out with a smile at the end of the show.

Safety

Ultimately, the Front of House is responsible for ensuring exits are kept clear in case of fire. Seating arrangements must be in keeping with safety regulations, and all the exit signs illuminated.

In general, the Front of House is responsible for the audience. There might be a bar, a cloakroom for coats, toilets to oversee (is there enough paper?). Snow may need sweeping from the entrance. Elderly audience members may need to be helped up steep steps and to their seats. Ticket problems may need to be sorted.

Catering

Catering may mean any of the following:

1

Simply selling chocolates or popcorn beforehand

2

Providing tea and coffees, ice-cream or savoury snacks in the interval

3

Supplying a supper or dinner

It is vital to ensure in the pre-planning that sufficient willing helpers are available to cover every performance and that the ordering of food and drink is taken care of in good time. Certain fresh products, obviously, will need to be purchased at the last minute but so long as thorough lists are drawn up and the buying delegated as necessary, this should present no problem.

Bars generally will require a separate staff and manager who will organise stock and sales.

Whether it is waiters and waitresses, or bar staff who are serving the audience, a cheery manner and efficient quick service are vital.

Try to select groups of people that get along well together and who are all willing to 'pull their weight'. As with all the backstage and front-of-house teams, it is working well together that produces the best results.

The ideal catering and bar staff:

1

Are good at preparing food or organising drink for large numbers

2

Able to handle money responsibly

3

Understand basic hygiene

4

Are familiar with health regulations

5

Can cope happily and calmly with the mad interval rush

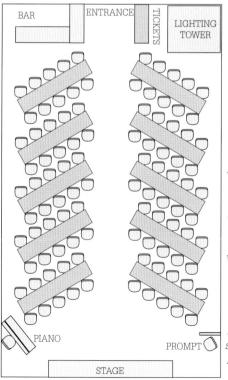

A 'cabaret' style of seating, with tables means that food and drink can be served. This creates a great atmosphere, especially if the tables are well-presented with tablecloths and flower arrangements

If narrow tables are used, the numbers are not drastically depleted. Here seating with tables is 100 and in straight rows 110. The audience will face the stage during performance and turn their seats around to the tables at supper-time! Generous aisle space must be allowed and the seating plans will need to be submitted to the local authorities for approval

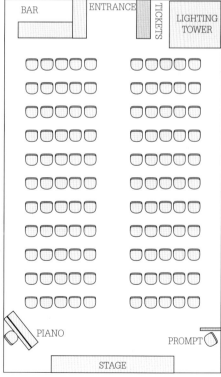

Other important help

Children add a great deal to a production and thoroughly enjoy being involved. The support of their families will boost ticket sales – but youngsters do need careful organising

Organising children

A good deal of extra organisation is involved when children take part in a production. They should never be left unsupervised or havoc may reign. Their exuberance can be difficult to deal with in a crowded dressing-room – especially on the opening night, when nerves are likely to make adults less tolerant of excited youngsters.

Also, in some cases, transport may be needed to fetch the children in time for the show or rehearsal, and to return them home again.

Often children become involved because their parents belong to the society. If there are several family groups involved, the parents might work out a rota between them, but otherwise appoint a responsible adult to take charge of them.

Make sure discipline is firm right from the beginning and that the children are never allowed to interfere in any way with the smooth running of the rehearsals or production.

Often dressing rooms in amateur theatres are mixed, with adults of both sexes in various states of undress. Children will need a separate space, preferably one where they can play quiet games so that they do not become bored. If there is insufficient space in the venue, see if the youngsters can be accommodated in a nearby house and kept entertained there. Runners can be sent to collect them in good time for their entrances.

The ideal children's organiser:

1
Likes children

2
Has good, firm discipline

3
Is patient

4
Is good at organising quiet games

5
Is sympathetic to the specific needs of youngsters

6
Knows the play's timing and the children's cues

7
Is flexible (rotas are subject to constant change!)

Someone needs to be responsible for:

1
Keeping the children quiet during rehearsals

2
Controlling them backstage during shows

3
Making sure they are ready for their cues

Co-operation

Co-operation between all the back-stage team members – and between them and the cast – is essential to the creation of a successful company. There will need to be a great deal of positive interaction between all these various backstage and front-of-house teams. Hopefully all the teams will help each other and find whatever balance works best for the production. In a small society, members may well be filling more than one role, but even when this is not the case, there is likely to be considerable overlapping of responsibilities and lots to discuss.

With a competent and enthusiastic team established, happy to co-operate and work hard together, everyone participating will be given great confidence in the show. The cast will feel assured that they are part of a professionally organised group and the entire production will gain momentum from this.

To ensure that all the teams work well together, try to achieve the following:

1
Establish clearly who is doing what very early on in the planning stage

2
Set up good lines of communication – such as lists of those involved plus their telephone numbers

3
Make sure there is ample opportunity for everyone to meet, not just at rehearsals but at planning meetings – and social events – when ideas can be shared

4
Provide rehearsal and backstage schedules – and keep all members in touch with any changes to these

5
Ensure the cast are aware of the backstage team members and able to contact them directly if need be

Responsibilities

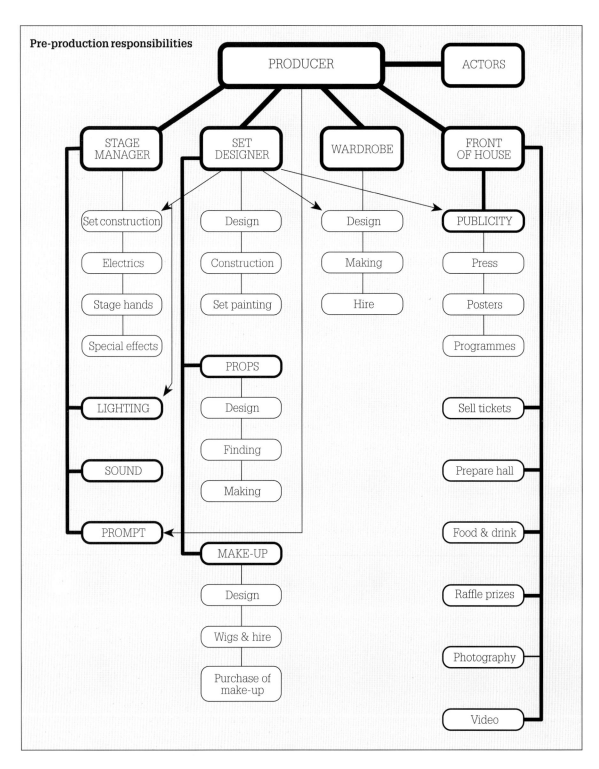

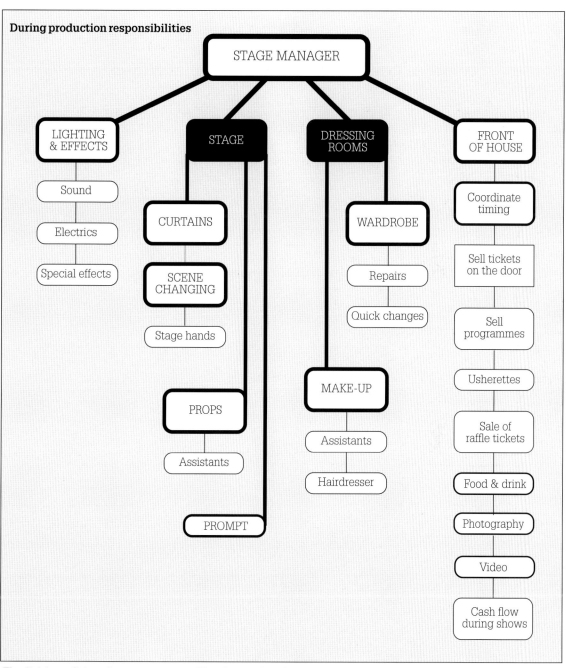

During production responsibilities

STAGE MANAGER

- LIGHTING & EFFECTS
  - Sound
  - Electrics
  - Special effects
- STAGE
  - CURTAINS
  - SCENE CHANGING
    - Stage hands
  - PROPS
    - Assistants
  - PROMPT
- DRESSING ROOMS
  - WARDROBE
    - Repairs
    - Quick changes
  - MAKE-UP
    - Assistants
    - Hairdresser
- FRONT OF HOUSE
  - Coordinate timing
  - Sell tickets on the door
  - Sell programmes
  - Usherettes
  - Sale of raffle tickets
  - Food & drink
  - Photography
  - Video
  - Cash flow during shows

The divisions of labour here display the conventional way that responsibility for a show is delegated

The chart on the left shows what happens prior to the production when the director or producer is in charge. The chart above shows how the responsibilities are transferred to

the stage manager once the show is into performance. The actors may also be organised by the stage manager then but this will vary from one society to another

Technical teams

Good planning

The actual techniques involved in a theatre production – set building, lighting and electrics and so on – are not the subject of this book. There are many excellent volumes on these technical aspects, including the other titles in this *Create Your Own* series but the aim here is to concentrate on the planning, delegation and organisation of these techniques.

It is vital that every technical aspect is handled competently and is well thought through. This requires each team to plan carefully prior to the production, to co-operate with the other technical teams throughout and to develop an efficient system in order to successfully manage the specific technical responsibilities during both rehearsals and the live show.

Each team will need to make cue sheets of one kind or another, while the stage manager is responsible during performances for co-ordination of all these elements

As a producer....
Working with all these technicalities can seem a difficult proposition – to co-ordinate all this and achieve the final desired effects without necessarily understanding all the techniques and mechanics. But even if you do not know your rig from your rostrum, being clear in your mind about what you want, communicating this, delegation and trust of well-chosen experts are the vital requirements rather than an encyclopaedic knowledge of how all these ends are achieved.

A few tips

Admit to your ignorance

Do not be afraid to admit your lack of understanding: if you do not follow something, say so – never pretend to understand or nod knowledgeably when you are in fact completely baffled by the jargon or technical wizardry. Ask questions; admit it is unclear. The others will generally be only too pleased to air their knowledge and explain.

Know what you want

Read through the script. Analyse carefully in your own mind how the scenes will look and sound, decide what you expect of the various departments – what effects you would like them to achieve in each scene. Make notes during rehearsals as further ideas arise. If you have duly considered these details and thought through all the possible decisions and consequences, then you will be in a strong position to discuss your ideas with the technical teams concerned.

Communicate

Having analysed your vision of each scene, communicate your ideas to each department clearly.

Listen and share ideas

While always holding on to the integrity of your overall vision of the play or particular scenes, do discuss, listen, share ideas and be prepared to consider the experts' suggestions and think again. They probably have lots to contribute. Do not squash any idea without giving it due consideration. Hopefully you will all inspire each other – for enthusiasm is highly contagious.

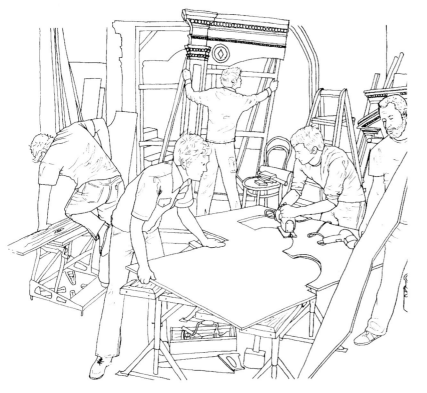

Stage management

Stage Management duties

Stage Managers will need to organise the following:

1
Security
Ensure all the necessary keys are available to open all required areas and that everything is switched off and locked up after the performances – unless there is a caretaker or janitor who oversees this

2
Communication
Keeping in touch with everyone throughout the performances

3
Marking the stage
The stage floor needs to be marked with slashes of carpet tape, like stamp corners, to indicate the positions and angles at which major items should be placed

5
Control of noise levels behind the scenes

6
Overseeing the scene and property changes

7
Overseeing special effects

8
Co-ordinating all the backstage elements
The aim is to ensure everything is done at the right time

9
Control of the curtain
Close co-ordination is needed with front of house, musicians and beginners to ensure a well-timed curtain up at the beginning of the show and at the beginning and end of each scene. An intercom is useful for this

The curtain must also be controlled during the finale and final bows. A finale must be planned carefully but the curtain timing will still need some instant judgement based on the audience response

10
Timing the performances
Try to keep track of pace and of when significant events occur. A chart made during dress rehearsals and then updated as the plot gathers pace will be a very useful point of reference

11
Dealing with emergencies
Keeping the show 'on the road' and the audience oblivious to any minor problems backstage – or, ultimately, calling the show to a halt if there is a major disaster such as fire!

12
Keeping everybody calm throughout

Stage Management

As described on pages 134 and 135, the Stage Manager (often referred to as the SM) takes over the managerial role from the producer once the play is into its final dress rehearsal stage. The responsibilities are wide ranging and depend upon the tradition of each theatre but, generally, the aim is to control the backstage team, to check that the actors are ready for their entrances, to check that the stage is ready for the curtains to rise – and to do one's utmost to ensure a smooth and problem-free production

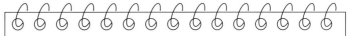

1 – Find out if props need any extra help on Saturday

2 – Have props managed to locate a garden urn?

3 – Check if we can keep the hall keys from Sunday onwards

4 – Remind everyone in opening scene need to arrive by 6.30 pm for make-up

5 – Organise dressing-room intercom

6 – Check smoke machine refills

7 – Confirm rota for stage hands all OK

8 – Move ladder

9 – Do 'NO SMOKING' notice

The sets

The sets

Set design and set building are not necessarily undertaken by the same person or team. Two very different sets of skills are required but if the designs and the practical implementation of these are to be carried out by two disparate groups of people then careful delegation and clear communication are essential.

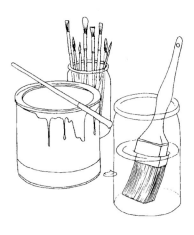

The basic kit

For set building, the following will be needed.

Saws

Jigsaw

Screwdrivers

Drills and bits

Hammers

Cutting knives and craft knives

Scissors

Clamps

Stapling machine

Nails in various sizes

Screws

Nuts and bolts

Hinges

Glue

Measuring tape

Jars for storage

Pencils

Rulers

Right angles

Plumb line

. . . and a sturdy pair of stepladders

For the painting, you will need to gather together:

Paint

Lots of brushes of various sizes

Rollers

Old margarine tubs or saucers to use as containers for mixed paint

Spoons and stirrers

Buckets

Loads of old newspaper to protect flooring and other surfaces

Masking tape for screening areas to obtain straight lines

Finding a set team

You will be looking for two kinds of helpers – those with practical skills, preferably with their own tools, to construct the set; and those with artistic skills to help paint the set

1
Decide how many people are needed to build the sets

2
Decide how many people are needed to paint the sets

3
Ask for volunteers

4
Draw up a rota

Factors to consider before beginning:

1
What kind of play is it? Assess the overall play. Try to understand it – discuss themes and concepts with the producer/director

2
Do you need to do any research? Dig out useful information and illustrative material

3
Basic plan
Work out a basic structure for the set

Plan of campaign

1
Plan and present ideas
Give a general overview of how the sets will look and work. Rough sketches may be all that is needed at this stage. A scale model will be invaluable for demonstrating and discussing ideas

2
Detailed design
Design individual scenes in detail. Decide on final colour schemes

3
Ordering
Stock check then order any materials required. Check on paint supplies and available colours

4
Set creation
Implement or oversee the structure and painting of the scenery, making sure that any delegation is carefully structured so that the sets work as a whole

5
Co-ordination checks
Check everything with all the other members of the backstage team so that there are no unforeseen complications or clashes

6
Check safety factors
The sets must be practical, safe and take into account fire regulations. Check everything is in working order and safe to use

7
Dress rehearsals and performances
Check the sets all work as originally visualised and that the right atmosphere is conveyed. Make any last-minute adjustments as required

8
Strike the set. Remove everything after the final night and store as required

For the construction work, it will be very useful if the volunteers can bring along their own tools. As with any carpentry, good tools are essential. . . . A new group may wish to buy a basic kit

A few practical hints

Set building rota

February is going to be a frenzy of activity. Please can you help on any of the following dates? You do not need to commit to the entire time - just an hour here and there will share out the workload and make all the difference. And if you can only manage to pop in with drinks and sandwiches to keep us going, that would also be appreciated!

Friday 5th	Help – and transport – to move scenery into hall 7-10pm
Volunteers and time/vehicles available	
John	9pm –10pm
David P.	7pm – 10pm
Julie	7.30pm – 10pm
Nigel	7pm – 9pm
Sandra	8pm – 9pm
Ray	7pm – 10pm

Saturday 6th	Work parties to build sets	9.30 am-6pm
John	Julie	
David E.	Gill	
David P.	Emma	
Bruce	Susan	
Helen	Henry	
Viv		

Sunday 7th	Work parties	9.30am-4pm
John	Grace	
Julie	Sheelagh	
Gill	Robin	
David P.	Henry	
Eric		
Richard		

Saturday 13th	Set painting	9.30 am-6pm	Technical run-through 6pm
David P.	Emma		
Richard	Sheelagh		
Julie	John (after 12 noon)		
Viv			
Lynn			
Gill (till 1pm)			

Sunday 14th	Finalise sets	9.30am-2pm
John	Peter	
David P.	Richard	
Sandra	Gill	
Robin	Nigel	
Sheelagh		

Set planning

There are some existing simple symbols to use when planning a set. Use these to indicate on the stage plan such items as windows, gauze, flats, doors, chairs, tables and so on You can, of course, devise your own and may, in any case, need to design some further symbols to suit the more unconventional items.

Building sets

Build and erect the sets as early as possible. Much depends on what other demands are made upon the venue, whether you are rehearsing somewhere else, and whether there is an alternative place where set building can be undertaken, albeit a private garage or room. Whatever the constraints, aim to complete at the earliest possible date.

A rota, such as the one shown on the left is a useful guide to what help is available. It also makes those who have 'signed on' feel obliged to turn up!

These simple symbols make the set plan easy to understand. In this case, the pivoting flats across the back allow for a fast scene change

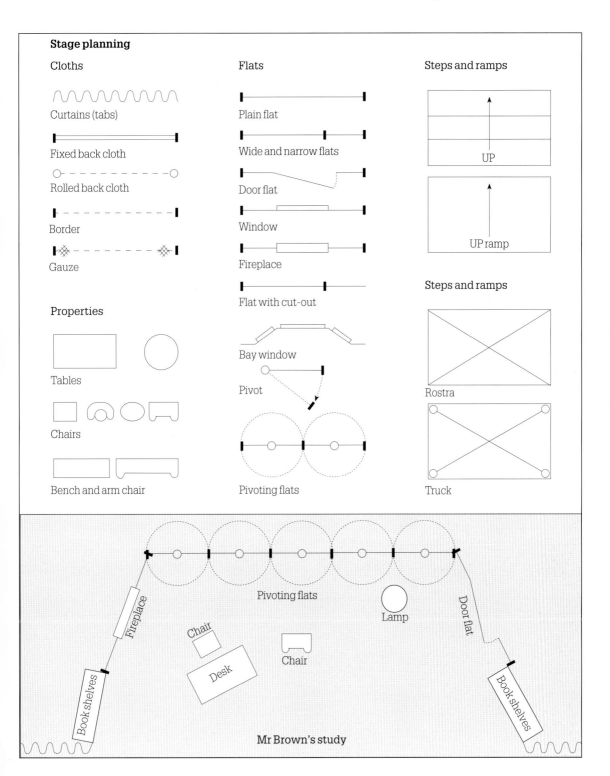

Stage planning

Cloths

Curtains (tabs)

Fixed back cloth

Rolled back cloth

Border

Gauze

Properties

Tables

Chairs

Bench and arm chair

Flats

Plain flat

Wide and narrow flats

Door flat

Window

Fireplace

Flat with cut-out

Bay window

Pivot

Pivoting flats

Steps and ramps

UP

UP ramp

Steps and ramps

Rostra

Truck

Mr Brown's study

Pivoting flats

Lamp

Fireplace

Chair

Desk

Chair

Door flat

Book shelves

Book shelves

A few practical hints

Scale drawings and painting

1 Scale drawings provide a good starting point for the set painting. Measure the size of the stage area to be painted. Do a scale drawing of the design and photocopy or trace this. It can then be squared up with a grid (like graph paper), with each square either one tenth actual size or one inch square.

2 Give the flats a white coat of paint first. This helps the colours used to be true and to have more 'luminosity'.

3 Once the flats are dry, use a chalk line to divide the area into squares. Mark both the scale drawings and the flats like a map grid – with numbers along the top and letters down the sides. Then transfer the designs. Reproduce a rough outline of the drawing, square by square, in pencil. Provide several copies of the squared-up design and several people can work at once.

4 The designer can alter or improve this guideline before setting about the painting proper. If time is short, helpers can fill in an outline with paint under the guidance of the set designer, like 'painting by numbers'.

5 Do not waste time on unnecessary detail. In most scenes, the attention is mainly on the actors. Finite detail will not be noticed by the majority of the audience. Overworking is especially wasteful if the stage is full of people. In a crowd scene, always concentrate on the areas above the actors' heads!

What to use

Water-colours or matt household emulsion paint are probably the simplest to use. Special colours can be mixed in do-it-yourself supermarkets or paint suppliers.

Rollers can be useful.

Set jargon

Flats
These are the basic stage pieces used for building flats. Long, tall and flat, they can be made from a soft timber framework with canvas, cotton duck, hessian, heavy-duty cardboard, gauze or muslin, or polystyrene. Composition board, blockboard foam board or MDF board may also be used.

Flat can be hung and fixed at the base. They can be built to make a room for a 'box' set. They may be swivelled or put on runners for quick scene changes. All the materials must be fireproofed before use.

A basic flat is usually constructed of 1 x 2 inch (25x50mm) frame and covered with canvas, sackcloth, hessian, plywood or hardboard

If made double-sided this can ease the problem of set changes

Filler flats
Apart from the basic flats, other 'filler flats' may be needed for special purposes, such as windows, doors, arches and fireplaces.

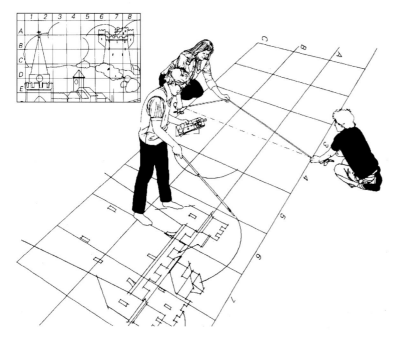

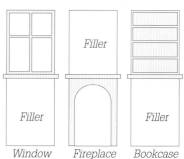

Window   *Fireplace*   *Bookcase*

A few practical hints

Wings

These are flats that stick out at the side at an angle. They occupy a lot of space so are not always ideal for a very small stage. Drapes or flats that 'box' the set with gaps for entrances can provide a great deal more acting area – but do make sure that the sightlines are screened.

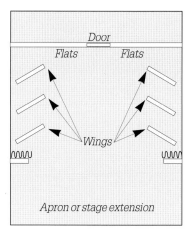

Ground rows and cut-outs

These pieces of scenery, often independent of the flats, can be used to establish quick scene changes or to hide incompatible pieces of equipment or staging such as a ramp, steps or lighting. Here a cut-out tree is linked to a flat.

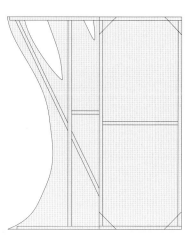

Rostra

These are raised areas. Split levels, blocks, platforms, trucks (mobile platforms set on castors) and steps of various shapes and sizes – both on the stage and leading up to it – add interest to the acting area.

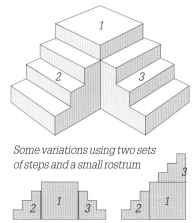

Some variations using two sets of steps and a small rostrum

A cyclorama or skycloth

This might be a smooth plastered wall or a stretched backcloth (curved or straight) which can be lit interestingly. Backcloths and drops can be hung and may be 'flown' if there is sufficient ceiling space above the stage and a sound safe structure capable of supporting the weight.

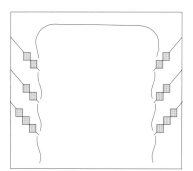

Cycloramas can be used straight across the back, curved or 'tented' around the stage

Gauzes and glitter curtains

Gauzes let light through and allow for transformation scenes and multiple ghostly effects.

Glitter curtains give a superb, reflective, shimmering effect. Different colours, as well as silver and gold, can all can be lit in exciting ways.

Perspective

This is a way of creating the illusion of distance. The designer must establish the eye level of the viewer. Is the audience sitting below or on raised seating? Where do you want their eyes to focus? Using parallel or converging lines will then create the effect of perspective.

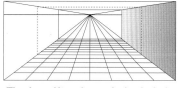

The dotted line shows the back cloth

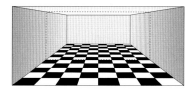

Lighting

Electrics and wiring are only for the expert. Professional skills are needed when handling such a dangerous source of power, but the actual use of the equipment, once it is all set up (rigged), is often undertaken by a well-trained amateur – and while the design must take into account the necessary safety factors, the overall planning requires artistry, imagination and a sympathetic response to the play, rather than just mechanical know-how.

Lighting guidelines

Aims

The lighting team will aim to:

1
Help visibility so that the audience can better appreciate what us happening on the stage and see everything clearly

2
Make sure all the stage is lit appropriately so that faces do not plunge into shadow

3
Add dramatic emphasis. Make creative use of colour and light to underline the plot

4
Establish time, place and weather. The time of day, the setting (such as a moonlit bay) and weather – such as snow, rain, clouds, thunder and lightning, can all be suggested by lighting

Practical aspects

1
Will any specially set lanterns or spots be required?

2
Is the current lighting rig able to meet the immediate requirements of the production?

3
Does any new equipment need to be bought or hired to achieve the desired effects?

4
How much power supply is available?

5
Where are the actors standing in each scene?

6
Which other parts of the stage need to be lit, and how?

Design aspects

Major factors to consider are:

1
What is the overall style of the play?

2
Is there any theme which can be helped by the lighting, for example, by colour schemes or the lighting of specific areas?

In each scene ...

1
What is the particular effect (or effects) required?

2
What time of day is it?

3
What is the weather like?

4
What is the mood in this scene (for example, happy or gloomy)?

5
Is this an historical, modern or futuristic setting?

6
Will a colour filter help give the right effect?

7
Should the lighting be realistic, moody or magical?

Lighting adds tremendous dramatic impact and can focus attention on a particular actor, group or part of the stage

Lighting

The lighting team's role will be helped if the following routine is established:

1 Assess the overall play. The lighting designer needs to be involved early on in order to plan ahead properly and work closely with both producer and set designer to achieve an integrated, smooth-running lighting plot and execution.

2 Plan and present ideas. Make a first lighting plan.

3 Research and experiment. This will help you to find out how best to achieve any special lighting effects such as a dappled woodland glade, a rainbow, a projected scene, a transformation scene and so on.

4 Check your plans. Confer with the producer and anyone else in your own, or other technical teams, whose opinion is relevant or who needs to know what is happening for practical reasons.

5 Plotting. Plot the lights in detail and work out cues. Make the lighting plot.

6 Run through the plan. Do this until it is very familiar. This will help you to stay calm and in control, especially if something does go wrong. This is particularly important for the novice

7 Attend rehearsals. Check out appropriateness of ideas and incorporate any changes into the lighting plot.

8 Stock check. Make sure you have everything you need. Order new equipment or organise hire, as required.

9 Co-ordination. Discuss requirements and areas of responsibility with electricians and any lighting assistants. Make a timetable.

10 Rig the lights. Check all angles and focusing.

11 Do all the necessary safety checks.

12 Technical run-through. Try out the lighting in situ and in sequence.

13 Make adjustments. Alter lights, fixings, angles, gels and so on, as necessary, and test everything again at the dress rehearsals.

14 Man the lights. Operate the lighting effects during the performances.

15 De-rig. As necessary, depending upon venue arrangements, take down lighting after show and return or store safely.

Lighting

Basic lighting angles and jargon

Front light

Flat front light is direct on to the face and flattens the features. It can be used to eliminate shadows cast by the eye socket but generally it is best to aim at a 45° angle from the stage floor which is far more flattering.

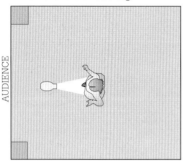

Key light

Provides the main source of light in any scene.

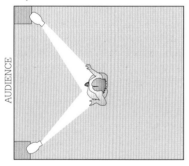

Fill light

This fills in any areas of shadow with a soft light.

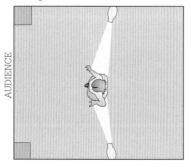

Side light

Helps to light the actors' faces when they face the wings and to give solidity and roundness to the face. Side light may also be used to suggest beams of sun or moonlight streaming on to the stage.

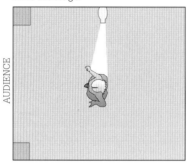

Cross light

This is a very shallow, or horizontal, side light.

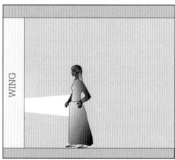

Back light

Does not affect an actor's face so is useful for filling background areas with colour. It may create a haloed effect around an actor.

Top or down light

Can be used for dramatic effects as it picks out certain protruding features, such as a wide brimmed hat, a pointing gun or a sword.

Bottom or up lights (or footlights)

These used to be called floats (from the days when oil wicks were floated on water or oil to avoid the risk of fire). Originally devised to show off dancers' legs, uplights give an eerie shadowy effect and they can be very dramatic for, say, lighting a villain. They can also be used to create low-level sky effects such as a sunset or horizon.

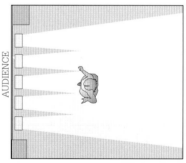

Types of lights and equipment

Profile spot

This very efficient lantern gives a hard-edged intense beam of light. Manipulation of the beam by gates and shutters allows it to be narrowed, concentrated, or less intense and with softer edges.

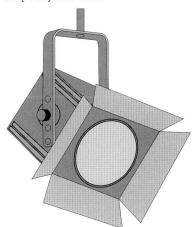

Fresnel spot

This creates a soft-edged beam with less harsh edges; the beam can be shaped by barn doors.

Pebble convex lantern

Similar to a Fresnel but with a convex lens which diffuses the light and makes the beam semi-hard edged and without flare.

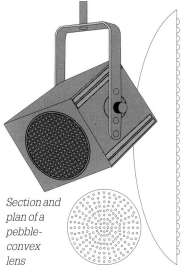

Section and plan of a pebble-convex lens

Par

Gives an intense parallel beam like a car headlight. It is good as a key light and for strong effects like sunlight.

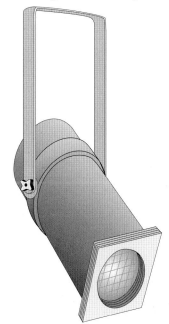

Flood

Covers large areas and so is excellent for lighting backcloths, on battens to form a strip or in ground rows as footlights.

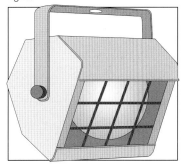

Gels

These are the colour filters once made of gelatine but now of plastic.

Control board

This is the 'nerve centre' of the lighting system, with all the various lanterns and groups of lights plugged into it – including the house lights in the auditorium. It generally contains dimmers which allow lights to be gradually brightened or dimmed so that different lighting effects can be gradually faded in and out.

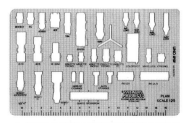

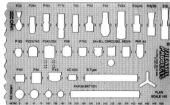

Symbols denoting the various types of light are used on lighting plans

Lighting

The basic kit

A new company, one whose budget is already stretched, or a society that has no storage space, generally opts to hire lighting equipment. If the decision is taken to purchase a kit, this can be done over a period of time, through several productions, and combined with hired equipment until a full complement is built up.

Try to acquire the following:

Four 500 Watt Fresnel spotlights

Two 500 Watt zoom profiles

One three-way dimming pack with an integrated controller

One 10-metre control cable

One tripod lighting stand

A six-lantern suspension bar

A safety plug which will detect any earth leakage and make the kit safe to use.

Cables, plugs and bulbs, barn doors and safety chains.

Obviously, the more lights you buy, the greater the flexibility of the kit and the more advanced the lighting effects can be.

If there is no purpose-built depot, both the lighting and the sound team may need to borrow, hire or buy scaffolding to build a tower or some other temporary but secure structure to provide a convenient vantage point with a good overall view of the acting area.

Cue sheets

When the lighting designer has finally decided on the lighting plot, all the cues and notes will need to be marked up on a cue sheet. This must be done very clearly so that it is simple to understand – even in a moment of panic – and so that the operating role can easily be delegated to somebody else if there is an emergency.

Lighting cue sheet

12 During interval make sure moonlight set up ready UC

Act Two Scene 1
The Dining Room 5am.

Curtains are pulled back from the French windows, which are open. Moonlight streams in.

Julia enters down the stairs. She crosses to the window and closes it. She draws the curtains across.

13 low light UR

Then she moves to the drinks cabinet and pours herself a stiff whisky. She opens the door to the hall, listens for a moment and then closes it again. Finally, she relaxes and sits on the sofa.

Enter Roger from the kitchen.

Roger   So this is where you are hiding. Did you really think you'd get away with it?

14 Cut moonlight + bring up 'dawn' lights ready for 15

Julia   What do you mean - get away with it? Get away with what?

Roger   Oh, Now don't try to be clever with me, young lady. I know exactly what you have been up to. I have been watching you very closely since Saturday night. You're clever, yes. You're devious, oh, yes – and you are also very, very beautiful.

Julia   Cut the crap, Roger. Get to the point.

Roger   Ah, the point! The point! Well, the point is, Julia, my love, that you have committed a very rare crime – a very rare crime indeed.

Julia   And what might that be?

She sips drink, trying to remain cool and collected but her fingers squeeze into the fabric of the sofa.

Roger   You have murdered a dead man!

Julia   *(rising)* Don't be ridiculous!

Roger   *(rising)* No, not ridiculous, not ridiculous at all. Very, very clever, in fact. You have more brains and far more courage than I gave you credit for, Julia.

15 Very low 'dawn' lights UC
He crosses to window and flings open curtains again.

Soon it will be dawn, and another day begins – another day as a lonely widow – but this time for real, this time, for the first time, no longer tied to that oh-so-rich but oh-so-boring husband of yours. You are free, my dear, free at last.

He crosses back to her and runs his fingers through her hair and around her neck, menacingly. Gradually bring up dawn lights during rest of scene

Cue list

12 UC Check moonlight OK during interval.

Bring moonbeam up just before act starts, as house lights fade.

13 UR Low light glowing in hall.

14 UR Cut moonlight as soon as Julia closes curtains.

15 UC Prepare pre-dawn lights before Roger opens curtains again.

16 UC Gradually bring up dawn light during rest of scene.

This is the first stage of marking up the script.

Once this has been done, list the cues.

The next stage will be to decide on the specific numbers of lights, their colours and the dimmer calibrations. Add these details to the Cue List once these decisions have been made.

Sound

Sound

The sound team needs to:

1
Understand the play

2
Plan ahead

3
Work well with the rest of the technical teams

4
Add dramatic emphasis – such as an explosion or a gun shot

5
Help to establish 'background' factors such as time, place and weather – for instance by a clock chiming the hour or an 'historical' wireless broadcast; the sound of sea and surf, traffic, or fairground music; wind or drumming rain

6
Give the play greater 'reality' – adding the fine detail to the play, such as door bells and telephones ringing, horses' hooves, trains arriving, water splashing. These might be taped or mechanical effects

7
Stay in control and keep calm

8
Contribute flair and fun
Whoever is selected to do sound needs to be imaginative, inventive and to have a good sense of humour

Sound effects can be created manually, as and when required, or pre-recorded and played back at the appropriate moment.

If the play involves musicians, they can help enormously too: a pianist and drummer can suggest all sorts of bangs, crashes, tinkling bells, and so on, while today's electric organs offer any amount of background and foreground sounds like waves washing onto a desert shore or harps playing.

Plan of campaign for organising the sound

1
Read play and highlight when sound effects are needed

2
Discuss requirements with producer and any other technical staff with whom you might need to co-ordinate (for example thunder and lightning would involve the lighting team too)

Check what music is needed for pre-performance and during intervals

3
Research possibilities on how to achieve effects

4
Make sound plot

5
Attend rehearsals to check out appropriateness of ideas and incorporate any changes or additions that occur into sound plot

Recorded sound effects

Using pre-recorded sound effects offers a huge variety of exciting possibilities. Sound effects can be created specifically and recorded in readiness or 'bought in' and mixed to suit. They are available on record, tape or compact disc in shops and libraries.

The advantages are the wider choice of sounds readily available, better audibility and a more professional final effect. If your needs cannot be met by an 'off-the-peg' sound, try

6
Borrow, buy, make or organise hire of any effects or equipment needed

7
If using taped sound, mix sounds as needed and make up tape with sound effects in correct order. Mark sound plot clearly with the final positions of each sound on the tape

8
Supervise sound effects at dress and technical rehearsals. Make any necessary adjustments. Finalise co-ordination with the stage manager and the rest of the backstage crew

9
Be there early on the performance nights – in good time to check everything is in order and to have apt welcoming music playing in house as the first members of the audience arrive

10
After the last performance, return any borrowed or hired equipment and store the rest safely away

Sound

manufacturing your own sound effect and recording this on to the sound tape for the play.

Remember to leave a decent gap between the various sound effects on your tape, to tape more than you think you need so that the sound effect never runs out too soon (it is a simple matter to fade it out when no longer needed) and to check the volume levels carefully in rehearsal so that you neither deafen your audience nor leave them straining to hear.

Basic sound kit

A basic sound kit can be gradually bought and improved as funds become available – or purchased as a package. These vary in price according to the amount and standards of equipment but usually cost several thousand pounds or dollars. A typical portable set consists of:

12-way mixer

Amplifier

Pair of speakers plus stands

Cassette deck

Compact disc player

Wheeled flight case for transporting kit

Microphones and stands

Cable, plugs and electrical fitments.

For recording in a studio you will also need:

Reel-to-reel tape recorder

Editing kit

A stereo digital recording system will provide a neat system that is light to carry around, provides good digital sound quality and is simple to use.

Sound effect tapes or CDs

Although these can be borrowed from libraries, they are relatively inexpensive and it can save a lot of time to have a few 'in house'. Keep an up-to-date list of all the sound effects you have available and their source.

You will also need a good selection of music for pre- and post-performance. As with the play scripts, copyright may need to be cleared and permission granted to use the music chosen.

Cue sheets

When the sound team has finally decided on the timing of the sound plot, all the cues and notes will need to be marked up on a cue sheet. As with lighting, this must be done very clearly so that it is simple to understand, whatever the stresses of the moment – and so that the operating role can

Invest in good quality speakers

A multi-track system allows sound effects to be mixed on the spot

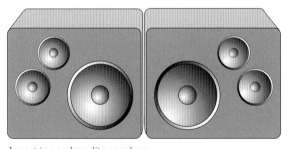

A sound mixer will help smooth the transmission of sound effects at the right levels

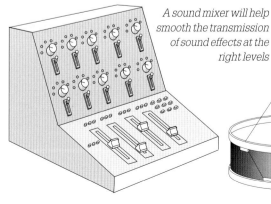

Simple sound effects

Rain and sea drum *Swish dried peas or lead shot around on drum or use sieve or hat box*

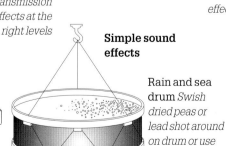

Glass crash *Wooden box with padding inside*

easily be delegated to somebody else if there is an emergency. Remember to allow plenty of lead time. Practise as often as you can during rehearsals so that you fine-tune the timing and are very familiar with the routine this play demands. Often the effects do not occur sufficiently frequently to require the constant attention of somebody in the wings and so the effects may be contrived by:

Stage manager

Lighting team

Sound team

Props crew, or . . .

A combination of them all.

If a specific person undertakes the responsibility, they may just come backstage as needed, under the stage manager's jurisdiction.

However, if pyrotechnics are being implemented, it is essential to employ a professional who can handle these potentially dangerous effects safely.

Ensure when you mark up a play script that you mark clearly not only the actual effect but also the moment when you need to prepare the effect in order to be ready in good time

---

Ensure echo microphones plugged in
▶ *Fade out 'house' music when S.M. signals*

Scene 1   Mission Control   *Cue sound effect 1 (count-down voices, explosion, and rocket take-off)*

House Lights fade fast so audience is plunged into a black-out. Curtains remain closed.

Mission Control personnel, in formal poses, all around auditorium, speak in loud thunderous voices.

1   10, 9, 8, 7, 6, 5, 4, 3, 2, 1, ZERO!

Loud explosion and 'take-off' sounds. Brilliant light flashes. Smoke swirls.

Voices
We have lift-off, we have lift-off
And it looks like a good one
Mission Cinderella is on her way; Spaceship Sentaprize is looking good, Sir.
Mission Control wishes to inform The Showman that launch is successful.

The Showman Calling Mission Control. This is the Showman. Congratulations!

Voices   Thank you, sir.
Cinderella is in outer space, Cinderella is in space.
And she's looking good.

Mission Control personnel on stage relax. Others break through from auditorium and join them. *Shouts also come from the lighting gantry .*   *Remember to shout !* ✱

Well done!
Super job!
Sock it to them, Mission Cinderella.
Three cheers for Mission Control! Hip Hip Hooray!
✱ Hip Hip Hooray!   ▶ *Remember to shout !* ✱
Hip Hip Hooray!

Song: Bye Bye Cinders

Cue sound effect 2 at end of song (Computer noises)

Scene 2   The Spaceship

Curtains open to reveal interior of spaceship. All is silent. All is still. In frozen animation, are the Cinderella-Hardup family, encapsulated in 'cocoons'. Slowly wheels
2 ▶ *start whirring, computers buzz, lights flash on and off. The ship is waking. Messages flash across screens, sounds buzz and crackle and entire ship lights up. A screen centre stage sparks into life and reveals the face of* **The Showman**, *a gauze transformation bringing his face into focus.*

The Showman This is The Showman calling. This is The Showman calling. May I introduce you to the only creatures still willing to participate in voyages of inter-galactic discovery, to go boldly where no man has been before. Only the most steadfast heroes of fairy tales will man our missions now, zooming into the unknown in frozen animation, to colonize new planets and take the message of true love and happy ever afterings to the rest of the universe.

Special effects

As with the sound and lighting, the special effects should be highlighted in the play copy and ideas discussed as to how these might best be achieved and whose responsibility they will ultimately become.

Generally the special effects will be included in the stage manager's prompt copy and allotted to one or various parties in the most suitable way, depending on whether the effect is being generated by lights, sound, props or pyrotechnics.

Useful special effects:

Dry ice
This is frozen carbon dioxide which produces a heavy vapour when melted in boiling water.

Smoke
Smoke can also be produced by special guns and machines. Apart from suggesting steam trains, clouds, fog, swirling mist and a fire in the vicinity, smoke can be combined with lighting effects to 'seed the air' and add to the effectiveness of light 'curtains' and beams of light.

Flashes and bangs
Maroons and flash powder are potentially very dangerous and a license is required before explosives can be used or stored. Moreover, such devices must always be implemented by proper, professional, trained pyrotechnics personnel. Small societies are generally advised to use pre-recorded sounds instead which can be made even more effective by shooting debris onto the stage!

Alternatively, professional photographic flash guns can be combined with coloured lights and smoke for exciting effects.

Snow
This can be suggested by various lighting effects or created by lots of paper dots or special stage snow released from a snow bag above the stage. This looks good as the 'flakes' float gently down but it is best used at the end of a scene or act so there is ample opportunity to sweep up the mess afterwards.

Ripple machines (or projectors)
These incorporate a tube into which ripple patterns have been cut. This rotates in front of a light source and creates gentle rippling waves of light, ideal for underwater scenes!

Bubble machines
Often used in discos, these are also fun for an underwater scene!

Mirrors
These can create flashing lights on a stage, just as the many facets on a spiralling globe in a disco have a fascinating effect. An hexagonal arrangement of mirrors revolving on a slow gramophone turntable and lit by a spot can flash across the stage and suggest, for example, the windows of a passing train.

Transparencies
These can help to set a scene and act as a backdrop on a darkened stage or be projected onto a more restricted area. They may be projected either onto the stage or at the side (which avoids some of the problems that arise when other lighting 'kills' the effect). Back projection may be considered to avoid interruption by objects or people in front.

The finale
Try to finish with a flourish. An exciting special effect can help give children's theatre, a variety show, cabaret, pantomimes, revue, music hall or the like a final touch of extra magic. Simple party ideas can also be very effective. Ticker tape streamers and party poppers will introduce noise and celebration. Masses of balloons can flood the stage with colour. Throw 'snowballs' into the audience, wave banners or tinsel batons or find other different ways to generate energy and festivity.

Special effects may need a cue sheet of their own if the show includes many of these. Most of the time, however, these effects will be incorporated into another department's plot. If a cue sheet is required, use the sound cue sheet as a guide for preparing one.

Quick change special effects

These can be achieved in various ways. Try some of the following:

1
Transformation scenes with gauze

2
Flats that are hung and can swivel

3
Flats on runners (like sliding doors)

4
Hinged flats (rather like an old-fashioned screen) with scenes on both sides

5
Layers of lightweight flats that can be quickly located on to pins on the main base flats

6
A trucked four-sided unit, with each face presenting a different scene

7
Canvas or material drops. These might be on a roller that can be dropped or might be flown. (Heavyweight cartridge paper which is used for photographic backgrounds can also be used. It is available in 9 feet (3 metres) or 12 feet (4 metres) widths)

8
Independent cut-outs can also suggest a scene in the simplest way possible and are especially useful in brief front-of-curtain scenes

Organising properties

Even the most simple play seems to involve quite a vast array of properties and stage dressing. It can seem an onerous task at the outset but is actually very rewarding, once everything begins to be gathered in and you can see the effect of all the hard work. The property department may be finding furniture, china, table linen, antiques, flowers, clocks, tree stumps and so on – or it may be making severed heads, swords, magic beanstalks, cakes, sandwiches, chain mail or flower arrangements. The range is endless and no two plays are the same.

The finding and making are just the beginning. Beyond that, the props staff have to keep everything in order, dress the stage, hand out personal props, change the props as needed for every scene, gather everything safely back into the fold again and then, when the performance is over, prepare for the next onslaught. To do this well a good deal of planning and organisation is required.

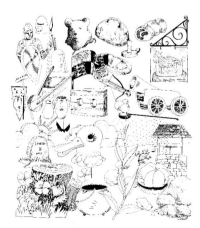

Properties are many and various. Making or collecting them is time consuming but very satisfying

Before beginning, factors to consider are:

1
What is the style and period of the play?

2
Is the property list comprehensive?

3
Does any prop present any particular difficulties?

4
Are there any fast scene changes that must be organised well in advance?

5
What will the different items cost to procure or make?

6
Is there anything already in stock that is suitable or that can be adapted?

7
Which props are essential to the plot and which ones are optional?

8
Who can help you to make the props?

9
Which, if any, pieces might be seen as part of the set design – or would require consultation with the set designer?

10
Will anything have to be hired?

11
What is the estimated cost of making or procuring the properties for this play?

12
What is the budget for properties?

Organising properties

The props department needs to:

1

Refer to and update the stocklist, showing the items the society already owns or to which they have easy access

2

Make a full property list for each production. The play copy's official list will form the basis of this but there are always variations and additions. The list should say exactly what is needed, when, and by whom

3

Gather everything in:
Ask the assembled cast if they have any of the necessary items or materials needed. Mark down on a list who volunteers what. Tick the items as located, delivered or bought – and note down after the show when each item is returned or has been added to the society's stock list

4

Make a plan of property positions

5

Mark up the play copy with property cues so that the requirement and movement of props is clear. Give yourself time to do everything with sufficient warning

6

Take care of everything:
Many of the items will have been borrowed. Props personnel are responsible for the care of these, as well as all the items belonging to the society. Precious items may need to be rescued from actors straight away and put back in the right place so there will be less chance of breakage or loss

7

Lay out all the properties so that they are ready in good time. A table for each act with the items presented in the right order will help enormously but if space is short there may need to be a system of rotation. Organisation is the key to success

Stocklist of props already belonging, or accessible, to the company

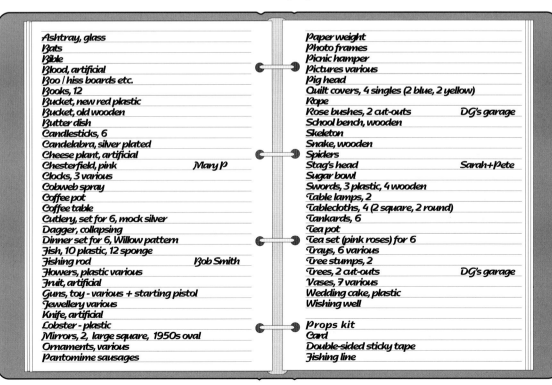

Ashtray, glass	Paper weight
Bats	Photo frames
Bible	Picnic hamper
Blood, artificial	Pictures various
Boo / hiss boards etc.	Pig head
Books, 12	Quilt covers, 4 singles (2 blue, 2 yellow)
Bucket, new red plastic	Rope
Bucket, old wooden	Rose bushes, 2 cut-outs DG's garage
Butter dish	School bench, wooden
Candlesticks, 6	Skeleton
Candelabra, silver plated	Snake, wooden
Cheese plant, artificial	Spiders
Chesterfield, pink Mary P	Stag's head Sarah+Pete
Clocks, 3 various	Sugar bowl
Cobweb spray	Swords, 3 plastic, 4 wooden
Coffee pot	Table lamps, 2
Coffee table	Tablecloths, 4 (2 square, 2 round)
Cutlery, set for 6, mock silver	Tankards, 6
Dagger, collapsing	Tea pot
Dinner set for 6, Willow pattern	Tea set (pink roses) for 6
Fish, 10 plastic, 12 sponge	Trays, 6 various
Fishing rod Bob Smith	Tree stumps, 2
Flowers, plastic various	Trees, 2 cut-outs DG's garage
Fruit, artificial	Vases, 7 various
Guns, toy - various + starting pistol	Wedding cake, plastic
Jewellery various	Wishing well
Knife, artificial	
Lobster - plastic	**Props kit**
Mirrors, 2, large square, 1950s oval	Card
Ornaments, various	Double-sided sticky tape
Pantomime sausages	Fishing line

Props Snow White	Who doing	Supplying	Found
PROLOGUE			
Sewing kit, needles & fabric			√
Stools or chairs		Ken L	
ACT ONE			
Chair		Susan M	
Small table or dressing table		Ken L	
Page 11 Crown jewels, long necklace		stock	
Cobwebs	Mary P		
Hand mirror,		stock	
Duster			
Page 14 Wooden pail		Bob K	
Page 18 Velvet spread			√
Page 20 Axe		Bob K	
ACT TWO			
Page 26 Beds	Chris D making		
Clothes, handkerchiefs		Mary P	
Pots		Mary P	
Warming pans	Simon B	hire from C & J Black	
Cups, plates		stock	
Books			√
Page 29 Working tools		Dave S	
Page 34 Wash tub with soapy water		Dave S	
Soup, soup bowls, ladle, . spoons	Mary P		
Page 41 Gag and Megaphone		stock	
ACT THREE			
Flowers on netting or wire		stock	
Basket of apples	Mary P		
Page 44 Cauldron	Chris D making	stock	
Page 45 Spell ingredients		Ken H	
Page 45 Red apple	Mary P		
Page 46 Garden seat		David N	
Lunch boxes			√
Page 48 Watering can		Susan M	
Page 48 Basket of green apples	Mary P		
Page 58 Coffin	Chris D		
Page 66 Presents and/or sweets	Mary P		
Page 67 Snowballs		stock	

Organising properties

Plan of campaign

1
Read play

2
Discuss ideas with producer and set designer

3
Research useful information and illustrative material

4
Draw up final lists

5
Mark up script with cues for cast's personal props, props needed in wings and prop changes on sets

6
Sketch out rough ideas for anything that has to be made specially

7
Check through existing properties

8
Discuss ideas with producer and rest of team

9
Ask cast and team if they can provide any of the necessary items or materials

10
Buy any materials necessary

11
Recruit and instruct any helpers

12
Make new items

13
Ensure these are approved by producer and/or set designer

14
Supervise props at dress and technical rehearsals. Check everything looks OK out front

15
Organise properties throughout performances

16
After show ... Gather in everything safely

17
Clean, repair and return items as necessary

18
Update stocklist

Props cue sheet

Check that:
Table & chairs on marks; bench at 45°
Cutlery set on table
Tray ready in wings
Richard has portmanteau

For this scene need:
Garden table, 3/4 chairs, rose arbour, bench, tray, tea-set, sandwiches, cake, cutlery, cake knife, portmanteau

Act One Scene 3
The Garden

Mrs West and Gertrude are seated at the garden table. A bench is stage left. Are SETS doing or us?

Susan enters through the rose arbour, carrying a tray set for afternoon tea. She places it on the table. + china, cake, sandwiches

Mrs West   Ah, so here is tea, my dear. Will you join me? Thank you, Susan.

Susan bobs a half curtsey and exits.

Gertrude   Why, yes; I should be delighted to indulge. It looks delicious. Thank you.

Mrs West   Do pour, Gertrude, will you?

Gertrude   Of course.

She begins to pour tea.

Susan enters again, followed by Richard. He is carrying a portmanteau.   Personal prop

Susan   Mr Richard, if you please, ma'am.

Gertrude rises as if to make a hasty exit but then recovers and sits again.

Mrs West   Richard, darling. What a surprise. And you are just in time for tea.

Richard   No thanks, Aunty! Still stuffed from lunch, what ho!

He lounges on bench.
I say, this weather is just the ticket, don't you think?

Mrs West   Quite perfect. Now do tell me all about this exciting scheme of yours. Gertrude has been filling me in but I gather she thinks you are quite mad!

Meanwhile, between shows, develop the habit of collecting anything that might be handy in the future or noting down the whereabouts of potentially useful items.

Useful materials for making props:

Cardboard

Coconut halves

Corrugated plastic

Cotton wool/balls

Doweling

Egg cartons

Felt and fabrics

Fibreglass

Flour and water (baked dough)

Foam board

Hardboard

MDF board

Metal foil, zinc and aluminium (aluminum)

Old containers, tins, bottles and jars

Paper bags

Paper or tissue

Papier-mâché

Plaster of Paris

Plywood

Polymer clay for small items

Polystyrene

Ropes and cord

Timber of all kinds

Upholstery webbing

Wire and netting

. . . As well as any useful scrap material you come across

Hints and tips

To help fast scene changes
Try to keep everything fairly light-weight but stable.

If props are static and not moved about during the show (say, a row of bottles and jars on a shelf) they can be glued on so only one integral item has to be moved.

Make plans of the stage and map out prop positions carefully, marking the stage floor with tape for fast but accurate positioning.

To save money and time

Be imaginative and resourceful
Keep outlines and any decoration or painting simple and uncluttered.

With the director's prior permission, ask the cast to help with simple repetitive tasks (like making paper flowers). while they are waiting around in between their rehearsing on stage.

Organising costumes

Organising stage costume

Obviously there is a good deal more organising to be undertaken with a large cast play – particularly a musical or a revue with numerous costume changes – than with a straight, small-cast play. The principles remain the same but, if the costume list is huge, allow more time and be prepared to delegate and oversee, rather than working in isolation.

Before beginning, factors to consider are:

1

What is the overall style, period, and 'nationality' of the play?

2

How will costumes help to establish character?

3

What colour(s) or colour scheme(s) will be most effective?

4

Is there a strong set colour to bear in mind?

5

Are there any fast costume changes?

6

What do you estimate the costumes will cost this time?

7

What is the budget for costumes?

8

Is there anything already in stock that is suitable or that can be adapted?

9

What features must be incorporated for the purposes of the plot?

Costumes List

Summer Punch

Initial costume list
November production

General comments
Set in 1990s
Summer
Normal 'middle-class' family and friends in renovated country cottage
Cast may have suitable own clothes but we must check colour co-ordination
Evening dress must look good and may need to be hired
June Hilary must be overdressed – OTT to impress
All characters in mid 30s, except Penny (aged 10)

Sets
Act One -   in kitchen and living room
Act Two -   Scenes 1 & 2 in living room; Scenes 3 & 4 in garden
                   Colour schemes yet to be finalised but probably as follows:
Kitchen -   white and pine
Living room -   brick red and deep pinks; turquoise sofa
Garden -   honeysuckle and yellow roses mentioned

Character	Actor/Actress	Act One	Act Two: Scenes 1 & 2	3 & 4
Emma Jones	Sue Pobbles	Casual separates	Evening dress	Jeans + top
Edward Jones	John Harris	Jacket and slacks	Dinner suit	Tidy set of shorts, T-shirt and identical dirty, torn set
Sally Pitman	Julie Glaser	Casual separates	Evening dress	Shorts, t-shirt
Penny Jones	Ruth Carr	Jeans + shirt	------------	Jeans and t-shirt
David Smart	Mike Pobbles	Casual separates	Dinner suit	------------
June Hilary	Jenny Davies	Smart dress	Evening dress OTT	------------
Teddy Redstart	Andy Carr		Dinner suit	------------

This initial list will be finalised later when set decisions have been made and actual garments chosen. It will help then to list the gaments 'in order of appearance' with script page references, shoe requirements, any quick changes noted and other relevant details, such as 'check if Props have matching handbag (purse)'
Tick off the garments as they are sorted

Organising costumes

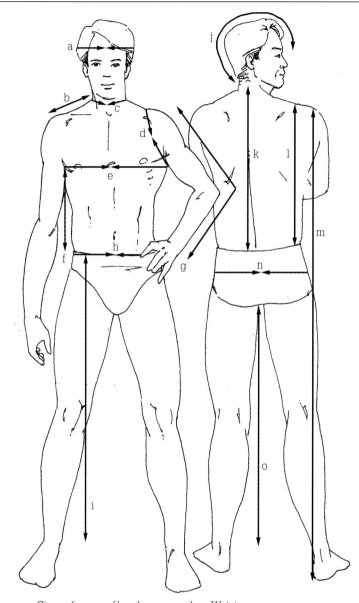

a	Circumference of head	h	Waist
b	Neck to shoulder	i	Waist to ankle
c	Neck (collar size)	j	Forehead to nape
d	Armholes	k	Backnape to waist
e	Chest/bust	l	Centre of shoulder to waist
f	Underarm to waist	m	Shoulder to ground
g	Outer arm–shoulder to wrist	n	Hip circumference
	(with arm bent)	o	Inside leg

Measuring and fast changes

It may not be necessary to measure every single member of the cast every time, if careful records are kept.

Always ask long-term members (tactfully) if there have been any significant changes since their last appearance and double check, anyway, if you suspect that there may have been! Be discreet: announcing to the world at large that so-and-so has shot up two sizes will not help that actor's confidence a jot.

Remember to measure heads in order to confirm hat sizes, and to note shoe sizes too.

Meanwhile, plan out exactly who needs which costume when – and which accessories. Note any very fast changes and be very well organized to smooth the passage of these:

Make a checklist of exactly what comes off and what goes on.

Lay out accessories and hang costume ready – in the wings, if necessary.

Undo any zips or buttons on the new costume, ready for an instant 'throwover'. Using Velcro fastenings will speed up a change enormously.

Organise a few practices so that both the actor and helpers know exactly who is doing what and when.

Have safety pins immediately to hand in case of emergencies.

If there is a large cast all changing at once, or a chorus line in identical costumes, label hangers and costumes clearly so that no-one take a wrong one in the panic.

Organising costumes

Plan of campaign

1
Read play

2
Discuss ideas with producer

3
Research useful information and illustrative material

4
Sketch out rough ideas

5
Check through existing wardrobe

6
Discuss ideas with producer and rest of team

7
Buy any materials necessary

8
Recruit and instruct any helpers

9
Measure cast

10
Make (or organise hire of) costumes well ahead of first rehearsal

11
Try costumes on cast

12
Alter as necessary

13
Work out plan of campaign for quick changes

14
Supervise costumes at dress rehearsals. Check everything looks OK out front

15
Be on hand during performances to help with any fast changes

16
Take a needle, thread, scissors and safety pins ready for any last-minute repairs

17
After show, gather in everything safely and then clean, repair and return items as necessary

18
Update stocklist

Drill the cast to hang their costumes up carefully afterwards, unless it is a very fast change – in which case someone else should be organised to do this.

Basic kit

Cutting table

Dress stand

Hanging rail

Iron and ironing board
(a sleeve board is useful)

Good source of light

Notebook and files for measurements and notes

Sewing machine

Storage containers

Zinc bath or bucket for dying

Haberdashery/Notions

Beads

Belts and buckles

Bindings

Braid

Buckram

Buttons

Chalk and soft pencils for marking fabric

Elastic in various widths

Embroidery threads

Hooks and eyes

Needles: heavy, lightweight, embroidery and sewing machine spares

Pins and pin cushions

Press studs

Ribbons

Safety pins

Shirring elastic

Tapes

Threads: a good variety of colours plus embroidery threads

Zippers

Materials

Clothes from secondhand sources

Curtains: velvet and net are useful

Fabric

Metallic foil

Newspaper, brown paper, tissue or tracing paper for making patterns

Sacking or hessian

Sheets

String and cord

Vilene or other stiffening

Wire – milliner's, fuse wire, garden and galvanised wire

Wool

Tools

Organising costumes

Cloths and sponges

Eyelet punch and eyelets

Hat block

Kettle

Measuring tape

Paint brushes

Pinking shears

Pliers

Riveting tool and rivets

Scissors

Stapling machine and staples

Thimble

Utility blades and knives

Yardstick

Other consumable items

Adhesives – collect a variety for different uses – including sticking fabric

Colour and metallic sprays

Fabric and leather dyes and paints

Scotch tape and masking tape

Hints about costume making

If dresses are made up as separate tops and bottoms they can be more readily adjusted to suit different performers on future occasions.

Make separate collars and cuffs to dress up basic, simple-shaped tops.

A variety of layers with overskirts, aprons and extra sets of frills and ruffles can dress up skirts to suit different situations.

Elasticised waistbands mean the costumes will fit a greater variety of

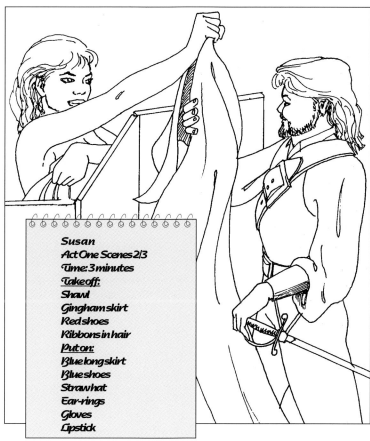

Susan
Act One Scenes 2/3
Time: 3 minutes
Take off:
Shawl
Gingham skirt
Red shoes
Ribbons in hair
Put on:
Blue long skirt
Blue shoes
Straw hat
Ear-rings
Gloves
Lipstick

Organising costumes

waistlines and are also very good for fast changes.

Using curtain tape on waists, sleeves and necklines mean these can be gathered in as tightly or as loosely as required.

Velcro fastenings help fast changes.

Make animal costumes from basic fur or skin-type bodies with interchangeable head-dresses or masks so that they are more versatile. If the actor has to talk or sing, make sure the costume allows for this and, in any event, ensure the actor can see clearly and be heard.

To convey a particular period or style, concentrate on the shape, the silhouette of the costume, rather than fussing over detail.

Avoid zippers, which can jam in a moment of panic.

Always organise the hiring of costumes well in advance to avoid disappointment or last-minute panics.

To save money and time

Make the clothes very simple.

Use lots of elastic and Velcro.

Do not fuss over details and finishing. The overall impression from a distance is what counts most.

Use fairly large stitches that can be undone easily if a costume must be altered to fit.

If time is really running out, hems can be glued.

Meanwhile, scour jumble or rummage sales for:

Baggy trousers (they can be converted into breeches)

Wardrobe department duties

The wardrobe department will need to:

1
Measure and clothe the cast

2
Ensure everything is ready for dress rehearsals, with time for alterations

3
Organise helpers if the cast is large

4
Oversee fast costume changes – or arrange for help to be available

5
Have an emergency kit backstage – scissors, thread, safety pins, Velcro, and needles that are already threaded up

6
Arrange for any borrowing or hiring of costumes – and for the collection and the return of these, plus any necessary laundry

7
Find any accessories – such as jewellery, hats, gloves, shoes, fans, handbags

8
Keep clear records of any costs involved

9
Keep a list of who has what costumes and accessories – and when and whether these have been returned

10
Make a plot of the play's costume requirements: the costumes needed, the times of changes, when fast or difficult changes are due and any other special needs

11
Keep an updated stocklist

12
Ensure costumes are stored safely somewhere that is clean and dry

---

Jewellery

Gloves, scarves and hats

Bags and purses, shoes, tights and other accessories

Cloaks and capes

Brightly coloured skirts and dresses

Curtains and bedspreads, furniture fabric and hessian, old sheets and blankets provide good material in bulk; net curtaining is invaluable for fairy tutus and wings, harem pantaloons and the like

Men's shirts (large white ones are especially useful and can be left white or dyed, and/or turned into jolly good pirate or musketeer shirts by adding full sleeves)

Evening gowns can provide useful sources of rich-looking material

Always save sequins, buttons, feathers, lace, buckles, ribbons, braid and trimming of any kind

Old fur coats (fake ones might be preferred) for animal costumes

Organising make-up

As with all the other subjects touched upon in this chapter, there is far more to discover than can be covered in this brief summary – so those whose field this is, are advised to seek more information in books that explore this fascinating subject in depth. If opportunities arise, try to attend some of the courses offered to members of amateur societies by both regional experts and such renowned sources of information as the Royal Shakespeare Company in the UK.

Planning ahead

The make-up needs to be well thought through and well organised. The play should be studied, the characters discussed with the director and with the individual actors, while a plan of campaign is devised for the performances.

Take into account how much time is required prior to 'curtain-up', who has fast changes and when, and at what points lots of people need help.

Then list the make-up needed in order of appearance. Decide which need expert attention and which can be managed by the actors themselves or by helpers. Define exactly where the pressure points will be due to mass attacks on a large number of cast at once, or for fast changes.

Costumes: "Who has taken what" List

Actor	Gear	√ when returned	Actor	Gear	√ when returned
John D	priest's robe sackcloth tunic cream tights rope belt		Nicky	yellow princess dress blue 'rags' dress Tania's wedding dress	
Anne	white medieval dress two-peaks hat blue cloak pink ball gown		Tony	blue doublet and hose navy velvet cape silver trimmed wedding regalia white tights buckled shoes	
Lynette	Queen's crown gold dress gold cloak white underskirt		Ruth	mauve fairy tutu silver shoes lilac tights pink wings	
Grace	witch's black robe witch's hat black cloak green tights		David H	red tunic brown cloak brown boots	
David E	brown leather tunic floppy felt hat cream apron silver tunic crown short gold cape		John F	blue medieval hat 'Robin hood' tunic plus tights rag and bone outfit	
			Sandra	pink striped dress white apron and matching hat	
			Susan	orange striped dress	
Angela	herald's red & yellow tunic red tights red boots		Lily	purple striped dress white bob cap	

Make-up chart for women

Production

Character

Actress

Base

Highlight

Shading

Powder

Moist rouge

Dry rouge

Lip colour

Eye make-up

Body make-up

Hair

Notes

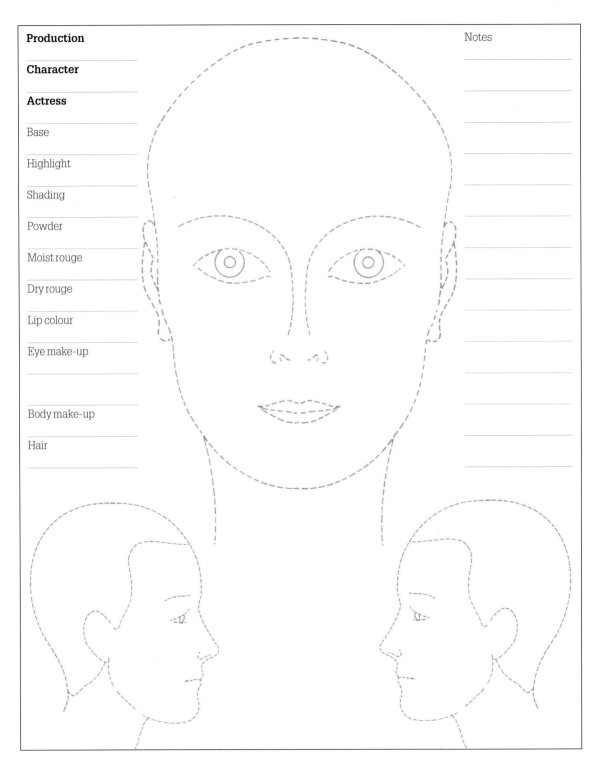

Production

Character

Actor

Base

Highlight

Shading

Powder

Moist rouge

Dry rouge

Lip colour

Eye make-up

Body make-up

Hair

Notes

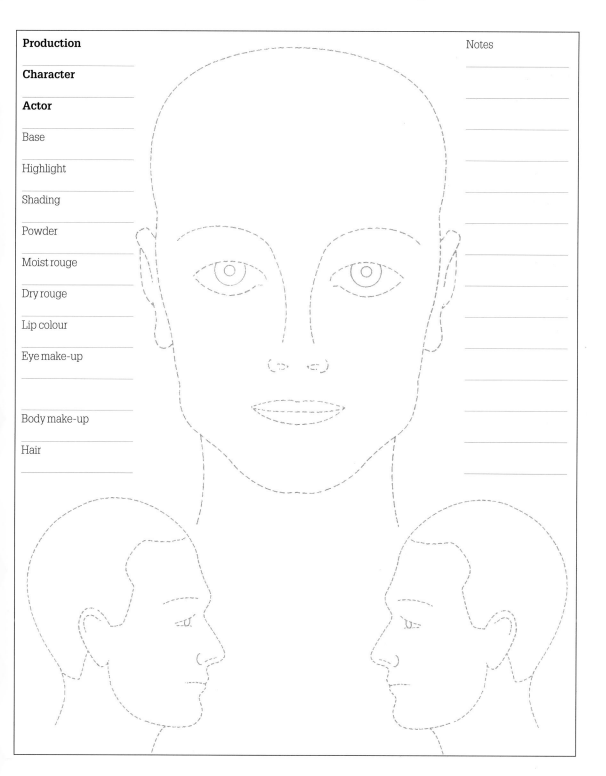

Organising make-up

The make-up team: aims

Organise stock control
To look after the make-up stock and buy whatever is required prior to each production.

Help define characters
Stage characters need to have an instant impact on the audience. Their roles must be complimented by the appropriate make-up. A whole range of age-groups and degrees of glamour and beauty or ugliness may need to be conveyed.

Instil confidence in the cast
Good make-up, like the costumes, helps the actors to feel their way into the role and to become quite different people from their everyday selves. If the actors are comfortable with the make-up, and excited by the changes they see in the mirror, it will help enormously to boost their self-confidence.

Counteract the draining effect of the lighting
Strong stage lighting can flatten the features and make skin colour paler so part of the make-up's purpose is to counteract this effect. It is therefore important to establish what lighting will be used when, in which colours, and just how powerful it is going to be.

Wigs and hair
The make-up person is responsible for hairstyles and may need to organise the hire or purchase of wigs, and to dress these if necessary – as well as helping with actors' own hair styling. Whether or not the make-up person can actually style hair or not varies from one society to another. The make-up person may act merely in an advisory capacity but it is a great bonus if he or she can organise professional help or actually style hair appropriately.

Beards and moustaches may also need to be made or applied.

Basic make-up kit

You will need:

Boxes with dividers to keep everything tidy

A selection of brushes, from fine eyeliner tips and lip brushes to plump rouge mops

Make-up remover and tissues

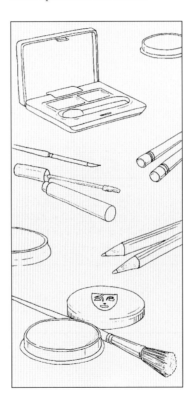

Cotton (wool) balls and cotton buds

Powder puffs

Foundations in various shades: these can be greasepaint, stick, cake or liquid bases

Sticks or pots of lining colours for adding detail

Rouge

Face powder

Eye shadow – powder, cream, liquid and pencil in a variety of colours

Mascara

Eyebrow pencils

Eyeliners – pencil, cake and liquid

Sparkle

False eyelashes

Liquid body make-up

Crêpe for false beards, moustaches, eyebrows and stubble

Latex and Derma Wax for special effects such as scars and warts

False fingernails (useful for witches and Eastern potentates)

False noses of various shapes and sizes

Nose putty

Spirit gum

Wigs and hairpieces

Black tooth enamel

Clown white

Stage blood

Scissors

Hair bands, grips and pins

Towels

Water

Obviously, the more specialised items will gradually be accumulated as the need arises. Many make-up kits are launched with just a few basic stocks of foundation, powder and cleansing cream, augmented by the cast's own make-up and left-overs begged from various sources. This initial stock will gradually be added to and replaced over the years.

Organising make-up

Factors to consider are:

1
What is the style and period of the play?

2
How will make-up help to establish character?

3
Does any particular character need research or special attention?

4
Are there any fast scene changes that will need to be organised in advance?

5
Who can help you to do the make-up?

6
Will any wigs have to be hired?

7
What is the estimated cost of the make-up for this play?

8
What is the budget for make-up?

Hints and tips

Use shadows and highlights
Much of the effectiveness of make-up depends on light and shade, on its sculpturing qualities, rather than just its colour. For example, lines alone will not age a face convincingly. Create the effect of sagging jaws, eyebags, creases, folds and wrinkles with shadows and highlights, first asking the actors to grin widely and to furrow their brows so that their own natural lines can be detected.

To black out teeth
Use proper black tooth enamel. Anything else will not adhere properly to the surface of a tooth and will wash or rub off.

Plan of campaign

1
Read play

2
Analyse appearance of characters

3
Discuss overall style and aims of the production and the essence of the individual characters with both the producer and the actors concerned

4
Research any necessary background information and how to achieve effects

5
Make plot of timing, noting any fast changes or when lots of people will need help with their make-up at once

6
Draw rough sketches of make-up for any special characters

7
Attend rehearsals to check out appropriateness of ideas and incorporate any changes or additions that occur

8
Check through stock and buy any new make-up required

9
Organise hire of wigs

10
Organise any extra help that may be needed and plan who is doing what when

11
Supervise make-up and hair styling at dress rehearsals. Allow ample opportunity to practise any specially difficult or previously untried types of make-up

12
Check effect out front and make any necessary adjustments. Finalise co-ordination with the rest of the make-up team

13
Be there early on performance nights. Allow plenty of time to make-up the masses for any grand opening scenes and to concentrate on any particularly complicated characters

14
Be well organised for any quick changes

15
After the final performance, tidy up and collect everything together, noting any items which need replacement, and returning wigs to hire companies

16
Update stocklist and faces file

Organising make-up and music

Ensure the make-up stays in place
Drawing a moustache on a face can look awful and is potentially disastrous if the actor has to play a love scene: he is highly likely to leave the heroine with a blackened face. Similarly too much foundation or lipstick can be deposited on costumes and faces so if the actors have an imminent close encounter, it is especially important to make sure any excess is removed beforehand.

Also, ensure wigs, beards, moustaches and false noses are stuck on very firmly, too. Do not skimp and leave the performers at risk of, literally, losing face in front of the audience.

Use optical illusions to your advantage

Horizontal shadows and lines will widen and flatten a face, while vertical ones will narrow and lengthen it

Lots of little divisions make a line look longer. In the same way, accentuating eyelashes with mascara makes eyes look bigger

Light areas always look bigger and dark areas smaller

Finishing touches

A little sparkle or glitter will add glamour to make-up

Beauty spots are great for Restoration characters

Temporary tattoos are now commonly available

Make scars from DermaWax

False noses have a dramatic effect and change a face completely

Do not forget to make up the neck and hands

Organising music

Every society develops its own individual character, evolving according to the tastes of the directors and active members. Some only ever perform straight plays so music is not a consideration.

Others specialise in full-scale musical productions. Some dabble in the occasional music hall evening but do not see their role as strongly musical. Whatever the degree of commitment, if music is involved at all, it will require the same level of good organisation, planning and practice as every other technical aspect.

Organising music

The musical director needs to:

1

Play the music and/or direct the orchestra

2

Teach the cast the music

3

Through thorough rehearsal, help the cast to give the best performance possible

Hints and tips

Finding musicians or an orchestra
Some societies hire professionals. If the orchestra or musical director comes through recommendation or has a good reputation, so much the better. Otherwise, check stage magazines and journals, and local newspapers, to discover what and who is available.

Local amateur orchestras or school orchestras may be very happy to join forces with your group for a production. Ask around.

Red tape

If using professional players, contracts and other arrangements will be subject to the rules of the Musicians Union in the UK and the American Federation of Musicians in the USA.

The Performing Rights Society in the UK will handle all the administration of music copyright, licences to perform and the collecting of royalties. Remember that obtaining appropriate clearance applies to using recorded music as well as to any live performances.

Some theatres take out an annual licence for the use of incidental and interval music.

Lighting
Ensure good lighting for the orchestra or pianist – even if only an angle-poise lamp on the piano. However, do remind the pianist or whoever is appropriate, to mark any black-out cues in the script so that the light is turned off at these times and does not 'kill' the effect.

Plan of campaign

1

Examine the music or score. Play it through

2

Discuss approach with producer

3

Practise playing the music until all the score is familiar

4

Hold first music rehearsal to introduce the music to the cast

5

Teach the cast the music through well planned rehearsals

6

Record the music so that the cast can practise at home

7

Hold individual rehearsal sessions with soloists

8

Adapt music or make any new arrangements as necessary

9

Help the cast to maximise the effect of the music and to polish up their performances

10

Play during performances

To sum up . . .

Sometimes it can be difficult to find sufficient numbers of people to cover all these technical fields as thoroughly as one might hope – especially with a new group. However, even with a small back-stage support team, if sufficient energy and enthusiasm are injected into every aspect of a production and the teams work well together, the 'stage is set' for success.

Ingenuity and inventiveness is far more important than having masses of expensive equipment and some of the suggestions included here should encourage novice producers and backstage personnel into appreciating just how much can be contributed by a keen and imaginative backstage team.

1

Think laterally

2

Be positive

3

Research, read books and drama magazines, ask questions, seek the advice of other societies

4

Experiment until ways are found to achieve the desired effects

5

Share ideas. Talk to other members of the backstage team and try to help each other as much as possible

Throughout, 'team' is the operative word. It is this pooling of expertise and enthusiasm to a common end – a successful production – that will turn the commonplace play into something really stunning!

Into Rehearsal

The play is cast. The backstage team is established and is already busy planning and preparing. Now the directors or producers are responsible for organising and running rehearsals – and the success of the show will largely depend upon their dedication and enthusiasm.

Planning the rehearsals

Being fully in control of the rehearsals from the word go is essential if the acting team is to remain co-operative. It is essential to maximise the use of everyone's time. Thinking through all the timing and structure of rehearsals, the moves (see pages 28-9 and 92) and the production aims will give the producer strength and confidence and inspire the rest of the team.

A rehearsal plan

A well-organised schedule will be the first stepping stone to good organisation. Copies of this should be ready to hand out to every member of the team immediately after the play cast is announced. The sooner the actors can enter the dates into their diaries, the less likely they are to have clashes of interest – and the weaker their case when trying to wriggle out of a rehearsal commitment!

Start with a blank calendar

First check the rehearsal venue availability. Then draw up a calendar with every possible rehearsal date so that all the options and permutations can be considered. These dates are the blank spaces into which you will slot rehearsal times. Make several copies of the blank sheet as it will probably take several attempts before the final rehearsal plan is to everybody's satisfaction. It is wise to check if any members of the team have difficulties with particular nights so that you do not plan to repeatedly rehearse their major scene on a night when they can never come.

Rehearsal dates

Hall is already booked out on:
Wednesdays - Line Dancers, Thursdays - Chess club
Youth club - every other Friday but finishes by 9pm
Other bookings, parties etc.

Golden Wedding	*Saturday 16 January 8pm*
Jumble sale	*Saturday 30th 2pm*
Birthday party	*Tuesday 9 February 4pm -8pm*

Teams:

Team A: Jack & Jenny, Mrs Brampton, Lena & Sir Henry, Fred Green
Team B: George, Julia, Count Drasticular, Dr Formula
Team C: Count Drasticular, Lady Fangtastic, Ms Siren, Lord Wolverine

January

Sunday 10	Read through – everyone	
Monday 11	Team A	7.30pm
Tuesday 12	Team B	7.30pm
Friday 15	after 9pm	Team C
Sunday 17	Act 1	7.30pm
Monday 18	Act 2	7.30pm
Tuesday 19	7.30pm Team A	9.00 Teams B&C
Friday 22	Music & crowd scenes	
Saturday 23	No rehearsal – yet!	
Sunday 24	Act 1 at 2.00pm	Music at 4.00pm

Monday 25	Act 2	
Tuesday 26	Act 1	
Friday 29	after 9pm Music	
Saturday 30	(Jumble sale pm) No rehearsal yet	
Sunday 31	2 pm Act 2	4 pm Music

February

Monday 1	Run through
Tuesday 2	Rough bits
Friday 5	Run through
Saturday 6	10 am work parties to build sets
Sunday 7	10 am ditto, 2 pm Dress rehearsal
Monday 8	Run through
Tuesday 9 - after 8pm	Rough bits
Friday 12 – after 9pm	Music & finale
Saturday 13	Set painting
	Technical run-through
Sunday 14 morning	Set painting
Sunday 14	**Dress rehearsal**
Monday 15	**Dress rehearsal**

Performances

Wednesday 17 to Saturday 20 February

Sunday 21	Clearing hall

1

With the diary dates listed, start pencilling in the vital rehearsals

2 Dress rehearsals

This sounds like odd advice but do not begin at the beginning. Start your rehearsal schedule at the end and work back. First fix the final dress rehearsal date. Whatever else happens, the performance dates are set and final rehearsals must culminate at that point

3

Try to leave one clear night between the last rehearsal and first performance so that everyone can draw breath and renew their energies before the show begins in earnest

4

Decide how many *dress rehearsals* you actually need. A minimum of two will be required to 'iron out' any problems that arise. Aim to have at least three full runs in costume, with all the props and scenery changes that are ready

How much of the technicalities can be included depends on the availability of the venue prior to the performances and whether or not costumes, lights and equipment are permanent or hired at the last minute

Even if the hall is not open to the cast until immediately before the show, dressed run-throughs elsewhere will still enable difficult costume changes to be evaluated and will help to speed up technical changes, if only by an improved awareness of the timing An additional advantage is that an early dress rehearsal may spur on the backstage team with their preparations and will certainly shock the cast into brushing up their lines

5 Technical rehearsal

Fix at least one *technical rehearsal* – two if possible

6

Now move back in time, slotting into the diary dates all the other rehearsals as follows:

7 Run-throughs

Over and above the dress rehearsals, it helps to have at least three or four run-throughs of the entire play, albeit undressed and unlit, during the last three weeks of rehearsal. This will help everyone, front and back stage, to have a proper understanding of the continuity and flow of the play and to appreciate how the timing relates to their particular role

8 Polishing rough areas

There are always some problem areas – perhaps a fight scene is very complicated, or a love scene looks unconvincing. This is inevitable – so always leave a slot somewhere in the last but one week for those sections that need special attention – for whatever reason

9 Music, movement and chorus or crowd scenes

Music rehearsals should be dotted throughout the rehearsal schedule. These rehearsals will provide invaluable concentrated attention both for the singing and for any choreography (of straight movement, as well as dance) that is involved

Whenever large numbers of people have to be moved around on the stage, whether for chorus or non-singing crowd scenes, this can take a good deal of organising. Allow a good proportion of time

10 Complete acts

Still moving backwards through the diary, plan when to run complete acts. Ensure that the time is shared fairly so that no one act is neglected.

If a particular act is especially complicated and requires extra rehearsal, the time share may not be equal – but should be correctly balanced to reflect the needs of the play. If Act Three is always left to the end of the evening, it will never be fully rehearsed

11 Introductory rehearsals

Now jump to the beginning of the rehearsal schedule in your calendar and pop in the first two or three straight rehearsals. These will involve the entire cast.

The aim is to familiarise everyone with the play and allow the plotting of moves

12 Working in teams

Depending on how the characters interact, it can be very useful in a large-cast play to divide the actors up into teams, say into four or five groups of people who always appear together.

While some characters may appear in more than one team, 'group' rehearsals can avoid a lot of hanging around for the actors in the early stage of rehearsals when the action is 'stop and go back' and 'do it again'

Planning the rehearsals

Absentee form

Absentees	(Let's have the good excuses then!)
January	
Saturday 7	*John in Germany*
Sunday 8	"
Monday 9	
Friday 13	*Susan leaving early (8.45) — David away*
Sunday 15	
Monday 16	
Thursday 19	
Friday 20	*Chris away*
Sunday 22	*on course*
Monday 23	
Thursday 26	
Friday 27	
Sunday 29	
Monday 30	**Sorry Gill - can't make it till 9pm love Tim**
February	
Thursday 2	
Friday 3	
Sunday 5	RUN THROUGH *Pianist late (Sue will stand in)*
Monday 6	
Wednesday 7	
Friday 10	
Sunday 12	DRESS REHEARSAL
Monday 13	*Prompt unavailable — find someone else!*
Thursday 16	RUN THROUGH
Friday 17	
Saturday 18	Technical rehearsal
Sunday 19	DRESS REHEARSAL
Monday 20	DRESS REHEARSAL

Other considerations

1

The rehearsal schedule will have to take into account such factors as the hall or the pianist never being available on Thursdays. While the permutations can become impossibly complicated if the producer tries to accommodate every actor's whim, try to spread each type of rehearsal over a variety of nights to lessen the impact of such difficulties. Only swap nights over if these prove totally impractical

2

Remember to mark in any committee or back-stage meetings to avoid double-booking

3

If times and venues are variable, do make it perfectly clear where each rehearsal takes place and at what time it commences so there is no possibility of doubt or error – or any excuse for argument!

4

Give the back-stage team copies of the schedule too

5

Print a reasonable number of extra schedules as some copies always go astray, and unexpected or new people will ask for them, too!

The absentee form can help the sensible planning of rehearsals. While one aims for full attendance at every rehearsal, there are bound to be occasions when somebody cannot attend. When this is predictable, it is better to be prepared in advance

Date changes

Try to be clear about dates right from the start. Adjusting things later on will inevitably lead to confusion. Accusations will fly and the organiser will be held responsible – even if the fault lies with the inattention of the actors concerned. Always put any essential changes in writing and make sure everyone has a copy.

Telephone tree

Despite all this careful planning, you may need to call an extra rehearsal or change the timing. You may need to cancel or postpone a rehearsal at short notice. Or perhaps you simply wish to invite everyone to a party!

Phoning every member of the cast and the back-stage team can be time-consuming and expensive. Using a telephone tree enables messages of any kind to be distributed, while sharing out the load and the cost.

It can be useful to ask the person at the end of each line of names to phone a central number and report when the final message has been received. This will enable the organiser to be assured that there have been no 'breakdowns' along the various lines of communication.

Make the telephone tree big and bold so it is less likely to be lost. Ideally, print it on the back of the rehearsal schedule or attach it to play copies.

The change of venue or time of a rehearsal, or its cancellation, need not involve any one person making copious telephone calls. Set up a telephone tree and give every member involved a copy. Then any information can be quickly disseminated throughout the team

Telephone tree

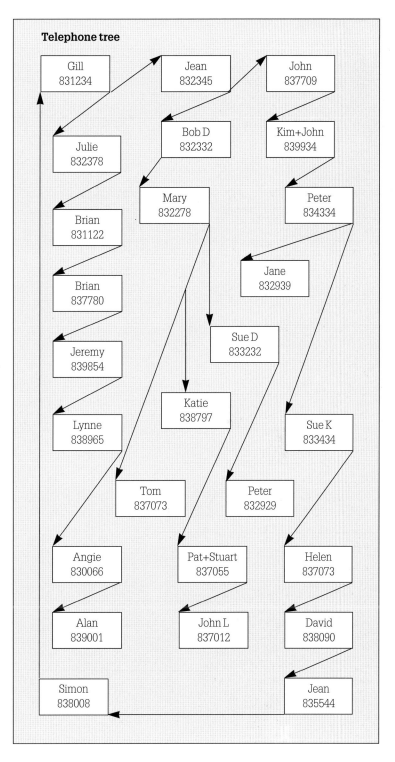

The first rehearsal

It is good to start with the full team gathered, front and backstage, so that everyone can find out all about the play, who is doing what and meet all the others involved. It will be a social event, not just a rehearsal, and this is of value because part of the fun of dramatic societies is forming friendships and catching up on news.

Order of play

1
Pep talk

2
Play read-through
or summary

3
Technical comments

4
Give everyone a chance to
express an opinion or response

5
Coffee break

6
Hand out paper matter –
schedules, telephone trees etc.

7
Ask members to fill in the
register (see page 88)
if they are aware of any
relevant date
complications

8
Introduction to music,
if appropriate

9
Social mingling; an
opportunity for the
producer to talk to individuals

The first rehearsal will establish in everyone's minds what is expected of them, what kind of production this will be and whether or not the experience is going to be enjoyable and worthwhile.

1 The pep talk

This first rehearsal is a prime opportunity for the producer to talk about the production, the approach, the aims, the timing, and whatever else is pertinent. It is the time to fire enthusiasm and to set goals. A good, lively pep talk to the general gathering should be followed later by individual chats with particular teams or individuals. Try to make everyone feel involved, special and important, no matter how minimal they might believe their contribution to be.

Be positive, happy and purposeful. Then, hopefully, each member will leave feeling excited about the production, committed to its aims and to his or her particular responsibilities. Ensure everyone is confident that this will be a brilliant show.

Stress the need to:

Attend rehearsals

Turn up on time

Learn lines early

Work together as
a team

Discuss openly any concerns
or worries

To work hard and to
enjoy themselves

2 Play read-through or summary

Some companies choose to read through the whole script with everyone in their actual roles. This helps to create an overall view of the play and the relationships between different actors. Much depends on the time available and on how often the play has been read during auditions. It may be felt that a summary of the play and its major points plus the reading of a few excerpts will suffice.

The main thing is to make sure the entire plot is understood by everyone before it is segmented up for the rehearsals that will follow next. *c*

3 Technical and backstage team

Try to encourage lighting, sound, sets, props and costume personnel to attend. Issues that involve them can be discussed in brief and the read-through or summary of the play will give them a greater understanding of its demands. It is a good chance for everyone to meet up.

4 Discussion

It is helpful for the cast to be able to talk about the play, both the general approach, important moments and the interpretation of each character.

5 Coffee break

This allows everyone to chat informally – which is often more revealing than the 'public' discussion!

*Provide newcomers with copies
of this 'areas of the stage' page to
help them become familiar with
the terminology*

Areas of the stage

Cyclorama

Wing

Up stage right

Up stage centre

Up stage left

Wing

Wing

Centre right

Centre left

Centre stage

Wing

Wing

Wing

Down stage right

Down stage centre

Down stage left

Extension or apron

The first rehearsal

The second rehearsal

6 Paperwork

You will be giving out scripts, rehearsal schedules, telephone trees, music and so on. Somebody must ensure that everyone has what is needed and that a clear record is kept of who has received what, or needs a missing item.

Tell everyone to write their names on their scripts straight away to ease the inevitable lost-property syndrome.

7 Register

Set up a 'register'. (See page 88) Have a diary of the rehearsal dates with lots of room for you and the actors to write down comments (or apologies) – if, say, they wish to bring a guest along, cannot make a particular night, or if the Press will be taking photographs on such and such a date. This register will continue to be updated throughout the rehearsal period.

Of course, it is to be hoped that there will not be too much absenteeism and part of the pep talk will be to impress upon the cast how vital it is to attend all the rehearsals, for the sake of everyone else concerned. But there are bound to be a few difficult dates so ensure these are duly recorded. Then you will be aware right from the start of potential problems – and able to plan accordingly.

Establish good communications

When you hand out the telephone trees, stress that communication is vital . Make sure that each person is primed to let you know immediately if he or she cannot attend or has a problem to discuss. Also that they have all the names, addresses and telephone numbers they need, over and above those on the telephone tree. For exam-

ple, if someone has volunteered to help organise wardrobe, they might need information about costume hiring companies.

8 Music

If the production has a musical element, this can be a good time to make a first attack on the music, with everyone there to join in. It will help to set the atmosphere for the show.

Talk to the pianist beforehand so that he or she is forewarned and has a chance to become familiar with the score (see also page 65).

Second rehearsal

Before this second rehearsal begins, the producer needs to have made a working version of the script.

If possible, take apart the script pages and put these into a file with the stage plans. Insert more empty pages so that you have useful space for notes opposite each page of the script and can see everything at a glance.

If you have not already done so at audition stage – make a note of everybody's height. Ask them to put this information in your register, if you like. Knowing their heights will be invaluable when grouping large numbers of people or pairing them up together for musical sequences.

Having set the ball rolling and fired enthusiasm all round, the next step is to organise all the moves. Depending on the complexity of the play, this may take more than one rehearsal There are two ways to do this:

1 Read the entire play, while blocking in the moves, or . . .

2 Walk through the entrances, exits and major moves – but without speaking the lines.

Blocking moves

Being organised

The producer will already have planned out the moves as described on page 94. Now these have to be tried out on the stage. Some are bound to change. Be open to new ideas.

Make sure everyone brings along a pencil and eraser. Take a few spares yourself for those who always forget. There are bound to be some changes later so it is preferable not to mark the script with a pen. If the play copies are borrowed or hired, they should not be permanently marked or defaced in any way.

As the actors go through the motions they need to write down the moves in the margins of the scripts.

It can be useful to bring along miniature plans of the stage to draw in any changes for your own records and to mark down precise positions of individuals in busy scenes. This will be much quicker than desperately scribbling down reams of words and will be easier to understand afterwards.

Stage terminology

Make sure that any newcomers are familiar with stage terminology. It can be very unnerving for beginners if they cannot understand any of the directions they are being given.

Provide stage plans with the terms and positions clearly shown – upstage, down stage and so on. A list of jargon such as tabs and aprons will be helpful too.

Jargon

See also Glossary on page 155-7

Apron
Stage extension projecting out at the front

Break a leg!
Good luck!

Darling
Term of false endearment often used by actors; sometimes used to refer to a showy, affected actor

Drop
Curtain or scenery, usually on rollers, that drops down from above

Dying
Forgetting lines and freezing on stage

An eye dropper
Containing stage blood concealed behind a knife blade is used to simulate cutting flesh

Flies or Grid
Area above the stage where scenery is flown

Fly
To suspend, usually above the stage

FOH
Front of house

Ham (or hamming it up)
Old-fashioned exaggerated acting (so-called because actors once used ham grease as a make-up base)

House
Everything beyond the stage

Legs
Long narrow strips of fabric, usually curtains at the side

Masking
Hiding someone or something

OTT
Over the top; exaggerated over acting or overdone staging

Personal prop
A small prop carried on or worn by the actor, such as a handkerchief, spectacles or purse. This is often retained by the actor between scenes, rather than being the responsibility of the props team

Rigging
Fixing up the lights in the venue as required by the production

Scissors
An awkward move when two actors cross each other on the stage

Sightlines
Point at which an actor can be seen by the audience

SM
Stage manager

Slapstick
Knock-about comedy: the term originates from the wooden bat that clowns or buffoons used to hit others

Striking
Removing a set or property

Tabs
Drapes or curtains used as scenery or to screen exits

Upstaging
Stealing the scene, often by forcing another actor to turn away from the audience

Washing
Narrow 'pelmet' of curtain that hides the lighting and mechanics above stage

Wings
Flats at the side of the stage to screen entrances. Actors are often found lurking behind these still 'mugging up' their lines

The second rehearsal

Making the moves work

To some extent this has to be a trial and error process. No matter how much thinking you have done at home, things always look different 'in the flesh'. None the less, all the pre-planning will have helped to establish the basic logic of the moves.

At this stage, the actors will still be clutching their scripts which limits their gestures and movement but this does not matter yet because you are concentrating on entrances and exits, the ebb and flow across and around the stage, and the positions where people will stop, stand, sit, lean, turn and pause. Some of these moves will change and mutate with later interpretation but this pattern of movement is the blue-print upon which you will build the structure of the show.

Make sure you avoid the following:

The traffic jam

This occurs when too many people try to move through an exit or entrance at any one time. Alternate the sides and the approaches. Stagger the moves as necessary.

Make sure the actors on stage are kept clear of entrances and exits about to be used and do not block another actor's entrance.

The crash

A frequent hazard at exits or while on stage. Ensure there is plenty of room to move and orchestrate the manoeuvres to avoid collision courses.

Illogical moves

Remember what is supposed to be where off-stage – so that continuity and logic are maintained. Ensure all the actors are aware of the 'geography' of the world represented beyond the visible stage. Are they aware which exit leads to the front door, or the garden, or the castle drawbridge?

Walking through the fittings

Furniture, walls and scenery are highly unlikely to be in place at the earliest rehearsals so use whatever is at hand to establish the necessary barriers, places to sit and entrances to pass through. Chalk can also be used to indicate distinct areas.

Forgetting to use the whole stage

Rehearsals ingrain information into the actor's brain; if they have always moved in a particular manner it will soon become semi-automatic and hard to override later. So remember to take into account all the different areas that are available right from the beginning. Similarly, do not overestimate the space available if the stage is smaller than the rehearsal room.

Even when the rehearsal stage is the one for the performances, some actors tend to hang about at the back or hog the front. Make sure there is a good variety of movement and that all the stage is used appropriately.

Upstaging

Upstaging can be an unconscious act or result from bad direction. Make sure the position of one actor does not force another to have to turn upstage.

If, for whatever reason, this is inevitable or deemed desirable, do not prolong the situation; also, ensure that the upstaged actor increases volume to compensate.

Moves that look uncomfortable

1 Too much crossing of actors on the stage looks awkward, especially if one of them is speaking at the time.

2 Avoid hesitant moves and bobbing about. Make sure actors move with a purpose.

3 Using the wrong arm to gesture or indicate hides the body and looks clumsy: the actors should always use the upstage arm.

4 Turning in on oneself looks bad. Turning the right way soon becomes natural but novice actors can spin around like tops trying to 'feel' for the correct way to turn. The trick is to turn 'through' the audience, facing them first and then following with the body.

Make the moves look interesting

The moves must flow smoothly and have a dramatic value too. Carefully planned groupings please the eye and paint pictures on the stage. Try to make the moves and groups look interesting, balanced, and a true reflection of the situation being enacted (see also page 96).

The next stage of rehearsals

Having blocked in the basic moves, the next rehearsals should concentrate on individual sections of play, working with smaller groups of people in greater concentration. While keeping an eye on the overall pattern on the stage, the producer will also be helping individual actors to establish their characters and discover their relationships with the rest of the cast. Voice and interpretation should be thoroughly explored.

The next stage of rehearsals

Make the most of the time before it vanishes! These rehearsals should provide a solid foundation before the manic final stages!

Be thorough

When you feel something is wrong, correct it immediately; try the scene once more, make any adjustments and then run it again. This constant repetition not only helps to hone the scene to perfection, it will also help the actors to remember their moves and lines.

Learning lines

Once the moves are settled and familiar, the lines must be learned. It is much easier to act and move when the scripts are put down. Initially, there will be some regression, while the actors struggle for their lines, feeling insecure – so the sooner this stage is passed, the better. A solid chunk of rehearsal time without scripts will ultimately give the actors much more confidence in performance.

It is also very important for the actors to absorb the sense of the lines and how they are carrying the plot forward. Then, if they forget the actual words, they can 'ad lib' coherently.

Moves create a link and a stimulus to remembering the lines.

Tape-recording their scenes and playing this recording at every opportunity may help the actors learn both lines and cues (which can act like an automatic trigger for the words that are to come).

Repeat difficult patches where the lines fail repeatedly. The prompt needs to be in attendance now, helping the actors with their lines and to keep on track as much as possible – so that the producer is properly able to concentrate on his or her role.

Hints on how to keep the team happy

1 Maximise rehearsal time

Plan rehearsals well, with approximate timings for when actors need to arrive so that they do not have to wait around for hours.

While one scene is being rehearsed on stage, actors not involved can gather elsewhere, preferably in another room, and work through areas that need extra practise.

Keep everybody busy and working hard and you will have a fulfilled, happier team.

Make sure all the sections are given their due time and commitment.

Be fair.

2 Encourage the actors to think!

Help actors to find their own way into the part. Never insist on an approach that straitjackets the performer. Explore the possibilities together.

3 Stay in control

Discipline is essential. Someone has to be in charge! Noise levels must be kept down and every member should respect the others' needs. The players will need to be self-disciplined, to be aware of their responsibilities, to think ahead and be constructive.

If the producer is all these things then the cast and back-stage crew should follow this good example.

4 Be aware of potential problems

Try to be aware of undercurrents and 'feelings.'

Try to avoid inflaming any personality clashes.

If someone is having problems at home, some extra tact may be required now and then. So, without prying into private lives, keep the antennae raised for unexpected flare-ups or over-reactions.

Try not to overtire the cast beyond their limits.

Keep everybody informed, especially about any changes to rehearsal times or contents.

5 Criticism should be constructive, not destructive

Rudeness, sarcasm and impatience are all destructive. Build up the actors' confidence with suggestions and guidance. If an actor is having real problems, a quiet chat about interpretation will achieve far more than a public 'put-down'.

6 Maintain enthusiasm

Often the initial enthusiasm tends to peter out halfway through rehearsals. It is vital to remain enthusiastic and positive yourself. Don't be boring or bored or you will end up with a boring play. Build on what you have; improving, rather than repeating.

Change things when necessary, even if this incurs grumbles from back or front stage. Have the courage of your convictions. Constant stimulation and moving forward will compensate for any extra work.

The next stage of rehearsals

It will help to concentrate energies if specific rehearsals, or sections of rehearsal, can be dedicated to

1
Music and choreography

2
Children

3
Complicated crowd scenes

4
Line rehearsals

5
Finales and line-ups

Also, other special sections might need concentrated attention such as:

1
Fights

2
Slapstick scenes

3
Love scenes

4
A death scene

Music and dance rehearsals

Obviously these need to be organised with the help of an experienced musician or choreographer. Like any other rehearsals, they need to be well planned in advance. If it is hard to stop the flow in the middle of a song or dance, take precise notes of any corrections and relay these to the cast when the music stops.

Meanwhile, a good pianist and accompanist will be able to help teach the cast the songs, guide the singers through these rehearsals, point out when the notes or rhythm are wrong and generally support the producer throughout.

At the first music rehearsal, be prepared for the cast to complain that the key needs to be changed: the songs are far too high. Do not rush to accommodate them. Generally, by the end of the rehearsal period, with all the extra practise, most of the cast can reach the notes quite happily and may even believe the key has indeed been pitched lower.

Songs

Do tell the actors to learn lyrics early. Learning songs is as important as learning spoken lines. Watch out for actors who lurk at the back, opening and closing mouths but only pretending to sing – or hiding scripts in the back row. There can be a tendency for everyone to think that someone else can learn the words first and nobody, in fact, learning them at all!

It will help if you can:

1
Exercise the voices first with some scales

2
Do some breathing exercises

3
Record the accompaniment so that individuals can practise at home. It is also useful to have this recording on hand in case the pianist cannot come to a rehearsal or is late

Solos or duets may benefit from a private rehearsal with the pianist to provide a good foundation for later shared rehearsals and to give the soloists extra confidence. It also avoids the rest of the cast waiting around too long. These rehearsals might take place before the main rehearsal time or at another time and venue altogether.

Dance

If there is a local dance teacher who is willing to help, this can be enormously useful. The producer should talk to the choreographer first and establish just what is required. However expert the choreographer, the producer will need to approve the routines and bring to bear his or her knowledge of the play and of appropriate moves and chorus work – which are not so very different from a dance sequence. The intricacy of steps, the need to tie in closely with the music and the range of terminology will be greater but the overall aim is much the same as that of conventional moves.

In the same way, a choreographer may well be able to help with difficult crowd or chorus sections, even if no dancing is involved at all.

Meanwhile, always make sure that the dance routines suit the abilities of the dancers and do not demand too much of complete beginners. Keep it as simple as possible unless there are experienced dancers who justify more ambitious ideas.

It will help if you can:

Find somewhere with plenty of space

Allow everyone to warm up first

Repeat the steps until even the most inept dancers have grasped these!

Children's rehearsals

Ideally, children need to rehearse separately from the adults in the initial stages. Later, everyone will need to be brought together but this process will be simpler if the children have already been given some dedicated attention. Generally, everything that has been said about the normal rehearsals applies to directing children, but over and above this, aim to:

1 Begin and end at a rational time so that the youngsters are not kept up too late

2 Be firm: children respond well to fair discipline

3 Ensure the rehearsals are very well organised and structured so there is no opportunity for bored youngsters to 'run wild'

4 Talk to the parents and, if possible, involve them in some way: for example, in rotas for providing transport, 'baby-sitting' during the shows, making costumes or helping to provide props. They will be more committed and supportive if they feel part of what is going on

5 Make sure both children and parents have schedules and are kept in touch with dates and times of rehearsals and performances

Crowd and choral scenes

Crowd scenes can be difficult things to manage effectively, especially if the numbers of people are large and the stage is small. In addition to this, the greater the number involved, the more the risk of absentees and stand-ins having to act as substitutes. However, if the ground work has been done thoroughly, careful notes are taken

and the cast is supportive and adaptable, it is amazing how the jigsaw pieces do fit together once the full team is finally gathered!

Work it all out beforehand. It will be chaotic if you arrive at a crowd scene rehearsal totally unprepared. Draw up

Children enjoy music and learn quickly. Some individual tuition and voice training may be needed for solo parts

Special or extra rehearsals

the battle lines and strategic manoeuvres! With large numbers of people to control, you will not really be able to draw lines to represent all the details of routes. In many instances you will be moving actors as groups, which simplifies matters: treat the group as you would a single actor.

When there is a complicated criss-crossing of individual actors, make multiple copies of the stage plan and then mark positions, rather than routes – as related to dialogue or lyrics. Draw separately or write in words a note about any particularly complex routes.

Impress on the actors concerned that they must keep track of their own movements. It is easier for them to remember one set of moves than for you to carry thirty sets in your head.

As ever, you will need to adapt some of your plans. In fact, probably there will be a good number of revisions before the moves all interlock neatly, look good, fit the music and flow smoothly. Keep a clear note of all the changes.

It can help to give the actors numbers – digits take up less space on your notes and if there is a vital order in which the actors appear, it helps to be able to call out and orchestrate the entrances and flow.

Throughout all this, as you watch the stage, analyse exactly what the crowd are meant to be feeling and what they are adding to the dramatic element. Make sure the moves, the patterns of the bodies on the stage, individual expressions, voices and the overall feeling convey this feeling accurately. For example:

In a welcoming opening or a celebration- make sure everyone smiles

A bustling and busy scene needs lots of movement

Fear can be conveyed by exchanged whispers; looking over shoulders

Confusion or puzzlement can be suggested by shrugging shoulders, exchanging blank looks

An angry and threatening crowd should wave arms, shake fists, shout

An ominous gathering will be conveyed by sullen silences, frowns and knowing looks

However, make sure not every actor does the same thing at the same time or it will look ridiculous.

Try to:

1
Stay calm

2
Keep notes

3
Ensure the cast write everything down

4
Most important of all, impress on the whole team that crowd and chorus scenes are very important. Getting it right means everyone getting it right, not just one person, so it can take a lot of rehearsal

---

Good acting from the crowd or chorus will create a rich and effective tapestry on the stage.

Line rehearsals

Specific line rehearsals may also be called to speed up delivery, and reaction to cues. Run through either the entire play or whichever sections need concentrated attention. If the prompts can run these rehearsals it will help their understanding of 'sticky' patches and improve their relationship with the actors.

Final line-ups
Here are a few points to bear in mind

1
The cast must look happy and smile

2
Individual bows can be taken by actors or pairs of them – or trios. If so, make sure that there is a good continuous flow and that everyone knows the order in which to step forward – and where to go afterwards

3
When the actors bow all together, ensure that somebody whom every actor can see is appointed as the lead, so that he or she triggers a united response and everyone bows together

4
Decide if ladies are going to bow or curtsey so that they all do the same

5
Make sure the orchestra or pianist and lighting/sound teams are given recognition and a chance to bow too

6
The Stage Manager must judge the applause and when to close the curtains finally. The cast must hold their positions and smiles until the Stage Manager signals that the curtains will not reopen again and it is safe to disperse, kiss or whatever!

```
FINALE PLAN

SONG: A Snowshine Wedding

At end of song        Move to back and take one bow, led by Bruce

                      CURTAIN CLOSES

Clear stage           Then come back on to take bows as follows

                  1   Children    Up side steps onto stage . . .
                      Bow as follows
                      Stacey and Cheryl
                      Simon and JJ
                      Andrew and David
                      Jordan and Ellie
                      Micca and Vicky

Down centre steps and back to places in front of stage

CURTAIN OPENS

The following people (numbers 2 to 9)
Bow once, down steps and circle round to reappear back of stage,
collecting snowballs and balloons from the wings as you go.

                  2   Dancers
                  3   Ladies in Waiting
                  4   Snowmen and Santa Claus
                  5   Young Queen and the Guards
                  6   Dwarfs
                  7   Clock and Mirror
                  8   Wicked Queen
                  9   Snow White and Prince

ALL BOW AGAIN
APPLAUD MUSICIANS
APPLAUD LIGHT AND SOUND TEAM

ENCORE SONG            It's the End

On line                'Dreams can come true', leave stage and progress through
hall, waving to audience - smile!

When reach back, on last line of song turn back to face stage
to shout 'The End!'

                      CURTAIN CLOSES AS CAST SHOUT   'The End!'
```

Run-throughs, technical and dress rehearsals

Run-throughs, technical and dress rehearsals

Run-throughs

Although there will still be some degree of 'interruption' from the producer, one or two complete run-throughs are essential to establish pace, continuity and timing. This will help back and front stage to assess the flow and so be ready in plenty of time for their entrances and cues. For example:

Stage Management and Props can organise and set stage furniture and hand our personal props.

Sound and lighting personnel can judge the timing.

The cast will grasp the flow of entrances and changes.

Technical rehearsals

The technical rehearsal is very important. Ideally there should be more than one, to allow time to experiment and to sort out problems. Electrics, lighting and other stage technicalities need sorting prior to the final dress rehearsals, so that these in turn can run more smoothly.

For practical reasons – such as having to hire equipment and venues, these technical run-throughs are often last minute so should be well organised to make the most of available time.

A first technical rehearsal does not need all the cast, just the guidance of the producer and a few people willing to stand in the right positions so that lighting angles, special effects, scene and property changes, sound effects, curtain timing, and so on can be tested

and adjusted. The aim is to run through the technical aspects in order so that they will be properly co-ordinated, right from curtain-up to finale.

A second 'dry run' might use the actual cast but will, once again, be a quick flash-through of positions and cues.

This concentration of time on the

Technical rehearsal checklist

1
Opening and closing of curtains

2
Order of scenes and changes

3
Furniture and property positions

4
Entrances and exits for scene shifters and props personnel so that everything is so-ordinated and well planned

5
Double-check timing of fast changes

6
Normal lighting positions and cues

7
Special lighting spots

8
Other special effects and timing of these

9
Pyrotechnics

10
Sound effects and cues

11
Double-check complicated effects especially if several departments have to co-ordinate.

technical aspects lessens the frustrations which inevitably arise if the dress rehearsal is expected to meet the requirements of both the acting team and a back-stage crew that have not been able to use the stage before. It is difficult to keep everyone happy when the tensions are rising, time is running short and the needs of the different departments clash.

Dress rehearsals

Dress rehearsals cut through complacency and make everyone – front and back stage – aware of the imminence of an audience – so it is useful to have one fairly early, say two weeks ahead. This will help highlight any problems and establish how the costumes are coming along. Obviously, hired ones will not have arrived but it still helps to discover the gaps and see if alterations are needed and whether extra sewing help needs to be drafted in.

Final week dress rehearsals

A dress rehearsal one week before should include as many of the scenery changes as practicable, all the available props, lighting and special effects and make-up. The one week that remains will be invaluable in sorting out any problems that have arisen.

Fast changes of costume and/or make-up need practise to run smoothly. A team of helpers may be needed to assist some actors. Meanwhile, if this proves insufficient, there is still time to insert a little extra dialogue or business.

If these time-consuming dress rehearsals can be held on a Sunday afternoon and run into the evening, there will be more time available than an evening alone allows. Warn the cast and crew that this is going to be a

Run-throughs, technical and dress rehearsal

long rehearsal. Organise for the provision of refreshments or suggest each person brings their own.

When everything and everyone is ready, the producer should:

1
Let each act run

2
Only interrupt if absolutely essential

3
List your comments and deliver these at the end of each act

4
Keep clear notes of any action needed

Dress rehearsals can be very tiring and frustrating. Good organisation is the key to keeping enthusiasm going

GD   Rehearsal notes

ACT ONE

1   Generally . .
Very good - costumes and sets great, play very funny — BUT
Keep pace up
Faster on cues
Don't talk in wings
Concentrate!

2   Opening number. SMILE, SMILE, SMILE please. Air of gloom.
Some of you looked terrified!

3   Tony - bring the lights up much quicker. Gloria's entrance? She was
fumbling around in the dark.

4   Props - that yellow chair was too far forward. It caught in the curtains.

5   David- You keep forgetting that one line about the hat, so Gloria doesn't get the
right cue. Please get it into your brain by tomorrow. Oh, and you forgot to
bring the walking stick on. Props - double check on him tomorrow, will you.

6   The flappers dance — awful, really ragged. We'll run that again before
moving onto next act.

7   Prompt — come in much quicker. Too slow when Gloria froze.

8   Sophie's entrance doesn't work with that bench in the way - move bench further
onto the stage.

9   Phil - that costume looks hilarious. Jenny - Allow for laughter when he comes
on before you rush in with your line.

10   John - What happened to your first entrance? Why late?

11   Lynn - was that costume change difficult? Do you need a dresser in the wings?

12   Props . . . That book needs to be dusty. It looks far too new and clean - and
there weren't enough glasses. Phil didn't get a drink.

13   Costumes . . . Jenny's shoes look wrong. Any others available?

14   Jenny - couldn't hear you in the romantic bit. Speak up; don't be embarrassed.

15   Faster curtain at end of scene.

16   Raffle prizes - we need more! Please.....

17   Can you all check your names are spelt right in the programme before we run all
the copies.

The final dress rehearsal

The final dress rehearsal

The final dress rehearsal is usually held on an evening immediately prior to, or just a couple of days before the first performance.

There will be mistakes but try to keep everything flowing and happy. There will be some aspects you would like to have improved but try to accept the inevitable if changes are impossible. Instead, concentrate on those improvements that can be incorporated. Minor details need to be noted, of course, and corrected if at all possible. But do not overlook the good points too. Balance out the 'nit-picking' with clear praise where due – both to front and backstage staff.

As with the previous dress rehearsal, let the acts flow and comment at the end of each.

Individual discussions with any actors or technicians can also take place between acts or perhaps when there is a natural break for a costume or for a scene change.

A full coffee break will be an unlikely luxury at this stage. Try to arrange for someone to brew up and serve beverages to individuals as and when it is convenient.

Final polish

1 Ensure the show has a strong opening and a good end. One hopes that the middle will be good too, of course – but a great start gives the audience confidence and a dramatic final flourish is something they will remember as they leave. Emphasise this to the cast.

2 Rehearse the line-up and bows lots of times, too. It should not look like an afterthought and thus let down the whole show. And if you wish to have encores, practise these thoroughly. It is especially important to rehearse the line-up early in the evening if children are involved who may have to leave earlier than the adult cast – but it is, in any case, a good idea to do this at the start. The cast will be more co-operative when they are fresh rather than when they are shattered at the end of a taxing rehearsal.

Throughout the last dress rehearsal, the producer should:

1
Stay calm and confident

2
Stay in control and concentrate on what really matters

3
Make sure when the cast leave that they are optimistic and positive – not complacent but looking forward to a successful show that will reward all their hard work and effort

---

Order of play

1
Pep talk

2
Finale and line-ups

3
Run Act One

4
Comments to cast

5
Comments to backstage team

6
Run Act Two

7
Comments to cast

8
Comments to backstage team

9
Run Act Three (if there is one)

10
Comments to cast

11
Comments to backstage team

12
If necessary, re-run any disaster areas

13
Final positive pep talk

The final dress rehearsal

Final points to stress

1 Remind actors and backstage staff to keep clear of sight lines.

2 Tell everyone to be quiet, especially in the wings or near the stage. It is surprising how far sound travels.

3 Remind the cast to keep the play flowing, even if something goes wrong.

4 Smile! Unless this is a serious play or a tragedy, remind the cast to be happy up there – especially important for chorus work.

5 Maintain the illusion: Ensure the audience believe in the play and the world you are creating. Actors need to keep in character until completely out of sight and sound.

6 Keep the pace flowing: The cast must be fast on line cues, and on entrances. The stage must never be left empty!

Make sure everyone is 'giving their all', – just as important in crowd and chorus scenes as in individual roles. Start and finish with a flourish!

7 Ride the laughter. Remind the cast that the audience will be a new element and will affect the performance in many ways, not least of which is laughter. The actors will need to adjust their timing to accommodate this.

8 Maintain the pace. Be prompt on entrances, cues and responses.

The first-night audience deserve a polished show. They are not there just to practise on! A good dress rehearsal will be a firm foundation for success.

Handing over

The cast should be made aware that the stage manager is in charge from now on although the producer will be very much in evidence, of course.

Responsibility now passes directly to the cast and back-stage team. Now it will be up to them to make the most of the production.

Remind cast and backstage crew to consider others

1
Don't lurk in the wings and block entrances and exits.

2
Don't chatter or laugh near the stage.

3
Turn up in good time.

Thank everyone for all their efforts.

Wish them luck!

Publicity

Good planning

It is vital that equal amounts of energy and enthusiasm are injected into every aspect of production. It is all too easy to overlook the vital importance of good publicity – yet a respectable audience is paramount to the success of any production. Full houses mean a healthy budget and ensure that the cast and backstage teams achieve the maximum response for their efforts.

A good audience makes the time and effort spent on rehearsals, set-building and so on worthwhile.

In fact, realising the dream of lots of 'bums on seats' requires considerable planning and organisation. However full the houses at the last performance, no group should ever be complacent. It takes a lot of hard work to attract an audience in the first place – and then to keep their interest alive for successive productions.

Certain popular plays or types of theatre, like music hall evenings, or shows with and for children, will always have an assured following. Even so, it is better to drum up as much excitement as possible for every show. There can never be too much interest. To be in the wonderful position of having to turn people away because the house is full will ensure that those self-same disappointed members of the public book earlier next time!

Allow plenty of time

It is important to start organising the publicity campaign well in advance, especially with regard to any printed matter. No matter how often you do this or how well thought through, any printing project (a programme, especially) always takes considerably more time to put together and finalise than is ever anticipated.

Moreover, if you are using professional printers, they will require reasonable notice to undertake the work, time to check on paper stocks, time to make corrections – and so on. While the theatre company, in turn, will need ample time to look at everything carefully and to make sure all is in order before 'pressing the button' on the final copy.

It is inevitable that if this is all done in a rush that there will be mistakes. These can be costly. They may also cause hurt feelings – for example, if someone's name is misspelt, or worse, omitted altogether. Some errors may be disastrous – for example, if the

Checklist of requirements at a glance	Posters must include:	Tickets must include:	Programmes must include:
	Name of the group	Name of the group	Name of the group
	Title of production	Title of production	Title of production
	Author (often a requirement of the granting of license or copyright)	Day, date and time of performance	Author
	Venue	Venue	Days, and dates of performances
	Days, dates and time of performances	Concessionary rate if applicable	List of acts and scenes
	Source(s) of tickets (names, addresses – and telephone numbers if possible)	Seat number if applicable	Cast list and backstage credits
	Entrance price and any concessionary reductions available		Acknowledgements and thanks

venue or time are wrong or missing from the posters or tickets!

Good organisation and a longer publicity campaign can help to build up interest locally and means more notice can be given to the Press if you wish them to attend the show or to provide pre-production publicity.

Publicity campaign timetable

Week 1

Prepare Press handouts and newsletters

Check posters, mini-posters and tickets in hand

Week 2

Contact: The Standard

The Gazette

Radio Greentown

East-West TV

Over 60s club

Newbourn School

Post/deliver
advance booking forms

Week 3

Distribute posters, mini-posters and newsletters

Post/deliver complimentary tickets

Check banner being made

Week 3/4

Organise photography for Press etc.

Week 5/6

Press photographs

Hang banners

Update posters with slash banners if necessary

Press release information
must include:

Name of the group

Title of production

Description of play

Bullet points of show's highlights

Venue

Days, dates and time of performances

Source(s) of tickets (names – and telephone numbers if possible)

Advance information sheets for regulars
must include:

Name of the group

Title of production

Days, dates and time of performances

Venue

Source(s) of tickets (names – and telephone numbers if possible)

Deadline by which advance form must be returned

Advance booking forms
must include:

Place to indicate first choice of date

Place to indicate first choice of seat type, if applicable

Place for applicant to write name and address

Name of the group

Title of production

Place to indicate total cost of tickets

Address to which it should be returned

If the group accepts credit cards, include a place for relevant details (card number and type plus expiry date)

Posters

Members of the cast are generally willing to display posters, as are local shops and so on. These are invaluable advertising and will serve the following purposes:

A useful reminder

If the society has fulfilled all the follow-up of established support, posters serve mainly as a reminder of dates and times so far as this regular audience is concerned. If the audience has not yet purchased tickets through members of the group or a direct-mail campaign, the posters will act as the trigger to remind them to buy their tickets now.

Attracting new audience

Posters also serve to draw in some new audience, perhaps people who have recently moved into the area or who are visiting or who feel it is about time they sampled the efforts of their local group.

Mini-posters

Small posters are a very useful bonus. If the society can arrange to run off lots of, say, A5 posters, these can be left in the local shops, pubs and libraries for people to take home with them. The local newsagent might even be persuaded to pop them in the newspapers. They can be posted through doors by members (or members' children!) and stuck to members' car windows to spread the word yet further afield.

Points about posters

Legibility

Make it easy for people to understand all this information and easy to obtain tickets. If the poster is illegible or it is a struggle to find out just who is selling tickets, sales will be reduced.

Quality

The poster should be attractive and created with care. Its quality will reflect the attitude of the group. A well laid out, legible poster, carrying the right information will reap dividends.

Colour is important. The printing can be black or white but if so, make sure the posters are on a coloured stock of paper. Alternatively, areas can be filled in with bright felt-tip colours.

Pictorial elements are fun – sketches, cartoons or computer-generated

AVENING PLAYERS PRESENT

RAPUNZEL

Avening
Memorial Hall
7.30 pm
21 to 24 February

Beer and Wine Bar
every night

Box Office
enquiries
David Moyce
Telephone
0134 567890

Wednesday
21 February
Family Night :
Adults £4
Children £2

Thursday 22
to Saturday 24
February
Adults £6
Children £3
Free supper
included

A·NEW·PANTOMIME·BY·GILL·DAVIES

images will attract the eye if they are well-done. However, much depends on the sources and talents available. Bad drawing looks unprofessional and is best avoided if in doubt.

Do ask around within your group and their contacts to find out who has artistic talents or is good at lettering and handling typography. There may, for example, be a cartoonist in your midst who can depict the actual members of the society in a humorous way, or perhaps there is someone skilled in the drawing programme on their computer who can provide black-and-white and a few colour versions of an exciting poster.

Someone might be good at writing little jingles or lively copy lines to capture the imagination of the passers by.

Updating the information

As tickets are sold, it can be helpful to create small banners to announce to the public the latest state of play. This can speed up decision-making for those not yet committed. Slashes across might read:

'Saturday Nearly Sold Out!
Buy Your Tickets Now!
Only A Few Left!'

Durability

Posters that are displayed outside may be affected by adverse weather: rain may ruin them or they may be blown away in fierce winds. Someone should keep an eye on their state. Sodden, torn, defaced or lost posters should be replaced with fresh ones on a regular basis.

A few laminated versions will be useful and reduce this problem considerably.

Where to display posters

Members of the society who live locally will generally be very happy to place posters in their windows or places of work.

Shops are usually very willing to help, too. Most of them prefer A4-size posters rather than large ones which take up too much window or notice-board space. It is useful to make your own checklist for specific places that will display posters for you but as a general guide, try to distribute posters to the following:

Poster checklist

Members and friends of the society

Shops

Libraries

Schools and colleges

Pubs and restaurants

Garages (gas stations)

Village/town halls or equivalent

Sports centres

Mini-posters can be a great boost to the publicity campaign

Points to remember

An integrated approach to the printed matter

Always aim to have a cohesive approach to all the printed matter. Often it is the poster that is the initial document that will 'set the standard' for the rest of the printed material. The style of the poster should reflect the style of the production. The general design, imagery, lettering or typeface, the way the information is presented aesthetically (such as the use of colour and images) and the approach (humorous or dramatic, for example) should all work together to convey the feel of the specific production

This style must be retained throughout programmes, tickets and so on – even if these are created by separate people

In order to achieve an integrated approach, the tickets can be a reduced version of the poster with a few modifications

Points about tickets and programmes

Make sure that these are created on a decent weight of paper. Otherwise they will deteriorate very quickly. Paper that is not of a good quality will look creased and shoddy as soon as it is handled

As suggested with the posters, draw on local talent and resources. Reflect the overall style of the production and ensure that these other various elements of printed matter have an overall style

Tickets

Print the tickets on a different colour for each night for greater clarity. This helps enormously when selling. And make sure the day as well as the date appears so that no-one turns up on the Friday instead of the Thursday because they have misunderstood the numerical date.

A tear-off corner can be used to indicate a child or special category reduction.

Seat numbers need not be actually printed. However, some sort of numbering is essential to keep track of the numbers of tickets sold. Special machines that stamp consecutive numbers can be purchased. These automatically 'roll on' the numbers as you stamp the backs of the tickets. These might or might not be used as seat numbers, depending on the booking system of individual societies.

The advantages of pre-booking seats are:

It is an excellent incentive to encourage audiences to book early

Audiences do not need to arrive so soon to grab the best seats

Friends can be sure they will sit together if they book soon enough

There will be less disturbance settling the audience into their seats

The disadvantage is

Extra pre-planning and organisation by members and their ticket sale helpers will be needed – but generally this is worth the effort

Tickets will need to show the following information:

Name and address of venue

Performance day and date

Row and seat number, if applicable

Time the performance starts

Title of show (optional)

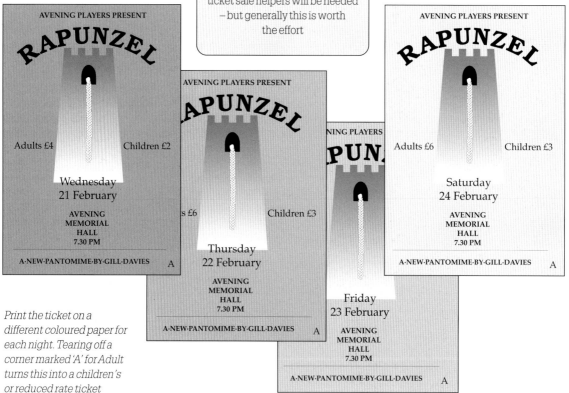

Print the ticket on a different coloured paper for each night. Tearing off a corner marked 'A' for Adult turns this into a children's or reduced rate ticket

Programmes

Make these interesting to read, not a boring or rushed after-thought that has obviously been 'thrown together'. Include a lively introduction by the producer, the author and/or the chairman of the group, conveying the 'ethos' of the production and the society. It can be fun to include also titbits of information about society news and what has happened during rehearsals.

Make sure the programme starts to 'sell' the show right away, awakening the audience interest with intriguing comments and lead-ins to the evening's entertainment. Set an appropriate atmosphere, welcome them to the evening in a suitable way, perhaps describing the setting – whether it be the streets of London, a Victorian household, A Midsummer Night's Dream forest, or a New York skyscraper.

You can also use the programme as a vehicle to attract new members. Include all the relevant names and telephone numbers to contact. If there are any other facilities on offer – such as society T-shirts or costume hire, the programme provides a fine opportunity to advertise such services or goods.

If possible, try to run off a rough copy of the programme about one week ahead. This can be passed around the members to check. This is a good way to catch errors, vital omissions or misspelt names. Most people immediately check their own entry and are quick to point out any error. Some may prefer a particular nomenclature (for example, Jimmy may prefer to be called James). Allow ample opportunity for several pairs of eyes to examine the programme before it is reproduced in large quantities.

The programme is indicative of the company's standards and approach so make it worthy of your group and your show

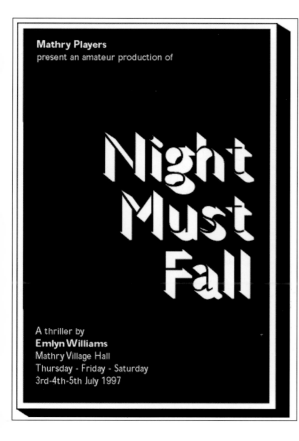

Programmes

Suggested lay-out of programme contents

Page 1

Front cover or Title page

Name of the group

Title of production

Author (this is generally a requirement of the granting of license or copyright)

Venue

Dates of performances, including the year (very useful when archiving!)

Price
(optional)

Page 2

Introduction

Optional but a helpful addition to the production
(often written by the director)

Page 3

The Acts

Acts and order of scenes

Interval timings

Any refreshment details

Page 4

Cast list

Usually in order of appearance

Pages 5 and 6

Backstage 'cast list'

This will include, as appropriate, some of the following:

Stage management

Lighting

Sound

Costumes

Musical Director

Properties

Make-up

Prompt

Set design and painting

Set construction

Stage hands

Banners

Tickets, posters and programmes

Box office

Choreography

Front of House

Refreshments

Production

The play was written by . . .

Page 7

Thanks and acknowledgements

It is important to remember everyone and make sure official gratitude is expressed for loan of furniture, seating, sale of tickets and so on

Page 8

End matter

Future productions planned

Invitations to join society or to be patrons

Information about props or costume hire if the company offers these services

Contacts: names and addresses of contacts within the society for future reference

Scattered throughout the programme

Local advertisements

If a small charge is levied for their insertion, this may help to defray costs

In a children's or holiday production, the programme might also include the words of songs or carols, if the audience are to join in with these.

Programme formats

Single sheet of paper – folded in half

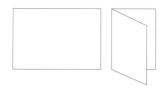

PAGE	PAGE		PAGE	PAGE
4	1		2	3
BACK	FRONT		INSIDE	INSIDE
COVER	COVER			

A single sheet, folded, is the simplest programme. Vertically folding an A4 (297 x 210mm) or 8 x 11 inch (204 x 280mm) sheet makes a programme feel different

If adding advertisements, it is easier to keep them all the same size. You can charge more if they are inserted in the front or back cover, but to simplify the design, try to avoid front cover advertising

– folded in half vertically

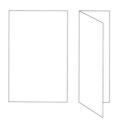

PAGE	PAGE		PAGE	PAGE
4	1		2	3
BACK	FRONT		INSIDE	INSIDE
COVER	COVER			

Advertisements can be added to the bottom of the pages

– folded zig-zag

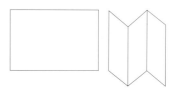

PAGE	PAGE	PAGE		PAGE	PAGE	PAGE
1	2	3		6	5	4
FRONT	INSIDE	INSIDE		BACK	BACK	BACK
COVER				COVER		

If the advertisements raise sufficient money to pay for the printing or photocopying and still provide a profit, you can give the programmes away. This is a good sales point for the advertisers as you can ensure that every member of the audience has a programme – and it is easier to calculate the number required. Do not forget the cast and crew will need a copy each

Two single sheets of paper – folded in half vertically or horizontally, making 8 pages

PAGE	PAGE		PAGE	PAGE		PAGE	PAGE		PAGE	PAGE
8	1		2	7		6	3		4	5
BACK	FRONT		INSIDE	INSIDE		INSIDE	INSIDE		INSIDE	INSIDE
COVER	COVER									

PAGES 2 + 7 ARE PRINTED ON THE BACK OF 8 + 1   PAGES 4 + 5 ARE PRINTED ON THE BACK OF 6 + 3

In the case of an 8 page programme, a little glue to stick in the inside is very neat; with three sheets or more a wire staple is required

Three single sheets of paper – folded in half vertically or horizontally making 12 pages

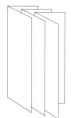

PAGE	PAGE		PAGE	PAGE		PAGE	PAGE		PAGE	PAGE		PAGE	PAGE		PAGE	PAGE
12	1		2	11		10	3		4	9		8	5		6	7
BACK	FRONT		INSIDE	INSIDE		INSIDE	INSIDE		INSIDE	INSIDE		INSIDE	INSIDE		INSIDE	INSIDE
COVER	COVER															

PAGES 2 + 11 ARE PRINTED ON THE BACK OF 12 + 1   PAGES 4 + 9 ARE PRINTED ON THE BACK OF 10 + 3   PAGES 6 + 7 ARE PRINTED ON THE BACK OF 8 + 5

If you wish, the cover can be a heavier paper stock

Remember when creating the programme, the odd numbers will always be on the left and the even numbers on the right

Programmes

PAGE 8 BACK COVER	PAGE 1 FRONT COVER	PAGE 2 INSIDE	PAGE 7 INSIDE		PAGE 6 INSIDE	PAGE 3 INSIDE	PAGE 4 INSIDE	PAGE 5 INSIDE
Next production and/or song Advertisement	Society Title By-line Place Dates Year	Advertisement Advertisement Advertisement Advertisement	About society Thank you's Why not join us Advertisement		Back stage team Advertisement	About the play Advertisement	Order of acts, scenes and when interval occurs Advertisement	Cast list Advertisement

PAGES 2 + 7 ARE PRINTED ON THE BACK OF 8 + 1   PAGES 4 + 5 ARE PRINTED ON THE BACK OF 6 + 3

This is a basic guide to the contents, but each play may be treated a little differently

Organising local advertising in programmes

Some societies ask local businesses to advertise in the programmes and use this as an excellent source of income. It should be appreciated, however, that attracting and keeping advertisers, as well as billing and collecting the monies due, takes a good deal of organisation. One or two members will need to specifically undertake this aspect and devote their energies to this end well before the time of the production.

As ever, a sound checklist of previous subscribers with all the relevant telephone numbers and contact names will prove invaluable.

It is vital to store carefully any artwork, logos or whatever the customer supplies for the advertisement – or that the designer creates. These logos might be kept as 'hard copy' or on a computer in whatever kind of file is applicable to the style of the artwork and/or computer program.

Depending on the style of the particular production, the wording of the advertisements might be adapted to suit the production – especially for a humorous play or a pantomime or fantasy. See advertisement on page 109.

Attracting advertisers is another reason for creating a good quality programme that is not instantly thrown away. It will be easier to invite local trade to advertise in something relatively substantial and retainable – and the revenue does help cover the programme production costs.

Sometimes societies are lucky enough to attract sponsorship from local business and this should not be overlooked as a further possible source of income. When this happens, it is very important that the sponsor is properly thanked in the programme.

Numbers of programmes

In the UK, where programmes are sold, some people never buy them. Of those who do, most couples and families share one between them. As a rough guide, reckon on one in three of your audience buying a programme.

However, do not forget that programmes are also a much valued memento for the participants. So allow one each for all those actively involved in the production, front and backstage. It is especially welcome if these can be presented to the cast and back-stage team on the first night so that they feel they have a privileged advance copy rather than having to grab an audience 'left-over'!

The number of programmes sold can be boosted if they are numbered – or have a raffle ticket attached – so that the lucky number programme can be announced later and a prize awarded.

If advertising has been included and has covered the costs of creation, it may be possible to give away the programmes free or make a very nominal charge. This pleases those who advertise as it guarantees a larger circulation for their advertisement.

Banner

During the week of the show, a banner over the venue or at a prime vantage point nearby will give the final flourish to an advertising campaign. It will remind local supporters that this is the actual week of the play, and act as a jogger to last-minute ticket sales and those on the door.

It also gives an additional boost to the anticipation of an eventful evening when people arrive. If the banner can be lit up this is an excellent way to lend it even greater impact.

Publicity control

Desk-top publishing

The society or group will often include somebody who has access to a type-writer, word processor, computer or desk-top publishing system of some kind, as well as photocopying services. If this is the case, programmes, posters, tickets and press releases can be created 'in house'. This helps to reduce costs but if the computer is in the office rather than the home, it may involve the willing contributor begging permission from 'the boss', working through lunch breaks or persuading someone else to help outside normal working hours.

Whatever the situation, it is vital to ensure that all the necessary information is gathered together as soon as possible to help those involved feel less harrassed.

Internal control can be very useful because programmes are especially subject to last-minute changes. There are bound to be some replacements and/or new additions, especially with

The arrival of the banner reminds the local audience that the show is imminent

a large cast or backstage team, and this is easier to cope with 'in house'. None the less, there is no reason why the basic information and structure cannot be brought together quite early to avoid any major panic during the final fortnight.

Publicity campaign

If one member of the group is responsible each time for publicity control, this will be the most efficient system. It avoids the learning process being repeated each and every time.

Moreover, regular contact with local newspapers, television channels, radio stations and so on can be built up and in due course will form a firm foundation for succeeding advertising campaigns.

Even just ferreting out all the names and telephone numbers takes considerable time. It is very wasteful if this information disappears between productions so, whether the role is swapped or not, do ensure a clean, updated copy of the contact list is kept on file for future use.

Press photograph for a production of The Crucible *by Arthur Miller*

Publicity control

Dwarves have bigger role in this production

AVENING Players perform a new twist on an old fairy tale this week in their production of *Snow White and the Seven Tall Dwarfs*.

The plot takes a turn from the traditional story when the dwarves grow taller after Snow White gives them some special soup.

Nicky Shipton plays Snow White, with Emma Chapton as her prince. Casting began back in November and the players have been rehearsing since January for this original performance.

The production takes place from Wednesday, February 23 to Saturday, February 26 at Avening village hall, starting at 7.30pm.

Tickets for the Wednesday performance are adults £5.50, children £2.50.

The remaining three performances include a ploughman's supper and are priced at £6.50 for adults and 3.50 for children.

● **Nicky Shipton and Emma Chapman who are playing Snow White and the Prince in the Avening Players production entitled *Snow White and the Seven Tall Dwarfs*** SMW197V00

JO BARBER and D
reporters on 01453 763 661 and

● Lynn Kellerman plays the clock while the wicked queen is Sue Burton in Avening Players' show.

Village's tall story about Snow White

AUDIENCES at Avening will enjoy a twist to a classic fairytale when they settle down to watch the village players' latest show this week.

Families will find themselves drawn into the specially adapted story of *Snow White and the Seven TALL Dwarves*, thanks to Avening Players' stage writer Gill Davies.

Co-director with Mrs Davies, Julie Sharpe, explained: "Gill always puts

a twist into our production. Another time we had *Cinderella in Orbit.*"

Mrs Sharpe explained that in the latest presentation, the dwarves eat a bowl of Snow White's food and grow to six feet plus tall.

Already seats for the performance at Avening Village Hall tomorrow and run until Saturday night, are sold out, apart from a few tickets still available for Thursday evening.

Some 30 to 40 adul children are involve White, which is Ave Players' 16th annua presentation.

Snow White is Nicky Shipton, as Prince Charming, while Chapman, while accomplished ca include schoo Townsend an Sir William R pupil Carey who are bot talents to w

● The young queen Julie McGuckin and her handmaidens

Photos: Simon Pizzey

The local press can add a great deal to the publicity campaign. Try to approach them well before the production to organise this

---

Around the Valleys

● Fabienne Bovis, Sue Werner, Bruce Franklin-Robinson, Gill Davies, Padhi Walker, Jean Franklin-Robinson, Michael O'Kelly and Patrick O'Kelly get into the right frame of mind before another performance of *The Scarlet Wimpernel*. (92-328)

They need seek him no more – he's in Avening!

Avening news

IT SAYS something for the growing success of the Avening Players that their eighth production – *The Scarlet Wimpernel* – was a complete sell-out.

For four nights the players performed to full houses and those who managed to obtain tickets had a real treat in store.

The play simply rollicked along, with plenty of audience participation, music, laughter and a lively can-can dance from several talented youngsters whose energy left older members in the audience gasping with envy.

The story-line was very loosely based upon *Alice in Wonderland*. Following a little green frog with a certain 'je ne sais croak' instead of a white rabbit, Alice crosses the Channel and finds herself in the middle of the French Revolution.

There she meets a delightful melee of characters – dandies and ladies of the court in superb 18th-century dress (Jacquie Biggs, was responsible for some very colourful and impressive

costumes), a group of frogs keeping fit at their croakrobics class, and several crazy personalities at the Mad Batter's tea party.

Ever threatened by Madame La Guillotine – a superb performance by Vivienne Moyce – with her accomplices Madame Defarge and The Executioner, Alice seeks the aid of the Scarlet Wimpernel to help her to escape through the Channel Tunnel back to England. In the event, she took the rest of the cast with her!

The sets were excellent – bright and bold rainbow colours, with a particularly effective Channel Tunnel scene.

The final transformation of Madame La Guillotine into Mrs Thatcher added a delightful twist at the end and was brilliantly enacted by Vivienne Moyce.

Contributed

Churches are blooming and it's thanks t

HILLTOP Gard meeting

Lib Dems ... or to ?

Rejection fou

Publicity control

The text for a press handout should be given to the appropriate editor or local radio and television broadcasters in good time for advance publicity

The main ingredients of the good publicity manager are enthusiasm and persistence – but a good helping of charm is enormously useful, too. It may take several telephone calls and letters to achieve the required result. Do not let your enthusiasm or positive manner be undermined by a long procession of calls. And, especially once you are through to the person who matters, make sure you positively bubble with the excitement of the production.

Whoever is handling publicity ought to be familiar with the play – sufficiently to promote the aspects most likely to attract an audience and interest the Press, or local television and radio stations. If not actively involved in the production, the 'publicity officer' will need to accrue a good base of information to begin their campaign. An informal chat with the producer may help to tease out interesting snippets. It is impossible to 'sell' a play if you have no idea what it is about! The aim is to capture the imagination of both the journalists and potential audiences.

Press hand-outs

Written material is always welcomed by the Press. It helps the theatre editor if his or her work can be lessened by the receipt of a well-prepared publicity piece. A letter can help convey the information in a lively manner. Always make sure that the main points are listed. A brief introduction followed by short snappy sentences and lists will work better than vast wordy paragraphs. Information presented in this way is far more easily absorbed.

If costumes can be organised in time, enclosing a photograph of the cast in action is another way to smooth the passage of the publicity campaign.

The Sunset Players present

A WILD WEST NIGHT!

Following on the great success of last year's music hall evening, to open this season the Sunset Players have decided to stage a Wild West show. This promises to be a great evening with a huge variety of acts, colourful costumes and plenty to eat and drink. Gill Miles who is directing the show, says, "As well as working hard, we have all had enormous fun rehearsing the Wild West night and I know that there are one or two members of the cast who will be loathe to part with their lassos and feathers! I am sure our great enjoyment during rehearsals will be translated into a good night out for all and so be shared with the audiences."

* Entertainment for ALL the family

* Songs and dance in abundance

* Funny sketches: masses of laughs

* Cabaret acts

* Supper included

* Licensed bar

* Our beautiful show girls will serve drinks at your table

* Don't miss the chance to enjoy a really lively evening.

Wednesday 5 to Saturday 8 January in the Town Hall. 7.30pm.

Other ways to promote the show

Even when the play is in a more serious vein, the same formula should work:

Other ways to promote the show

The Sunset Players present

NIGHT MUST FALL

by Emlyn Williams

This is a stunning play. The drama builds gradually and there are one or two moments that will be absolutely riveting. Seeing real drama live on the stage has an impact that no film or television production can ever equal. John Batchworth, who is directing the show, says, "Even in the earliest rehearsals with no costumes or scenery to create extra atmosphere, this play sends shivers down the spine. It provides an opportunity for some of our most able actors to shine and it has been very rewarding to watch the play and individual characters develop. The crisp dialogue and tense moments positively vibrate in the air. "

* A gripping play – murder and mystery at its very best

* Finely drawn characters and excellent performances

* Powerful drama and biting dialogue

* An unforgettable evening

Wednesday 3 to Saturday 6 February in the Town Hall. 7.30pm.

Please contact John Abbots Dry Cleaning (Telephone number) or members of the cast for tickets.

"What's On in Your Area?"

Towns and villages often publish a "What's On" pamphlet available in libraries or shops or distributed with local newspapers. Make sure your production is included in these regular publications. Check the deadlines for receipt of material.

Voluntary organisations

It can also be useful to contact charities and voluntary organisations who may be glad to bring a group along to the show. Much depends on the style of the production but senior citizens, for example, thoroughly enjoy an evening of light entertainment or a good thriller, while a pantomime or fairy tale is obviously going to provide an excellent evening's entertainment for a children's group or society.

Schools and colleges

It is worth looking at the examination curriculum, too, because if the play concerned – or its content – falls into this category then local schools may well be very pleased to bring a group along. In any event, it is worth contacting schools and ensuring they display the posters.

Newsletters

If the company circulates newsletters to its members and patrons, this can be an excellent vehicle in which to promote the latest production. The information can be conveyed in a lively way, amongst all the other gossip!

Keeping the campaign going

Timing of promotion

Always give plenty of notice to any newspaper or organisation.

Try to persuade the Press and local radio and television channels to give advance publicity at least one week before rather than a piece appearing half-way through the production run or even after it has finished. A good write-up afterwards is a boost for the society but is a bonus rather than a useful ticket-selling promotion.

Main publicity channels

Regularly update the contact list as shown at the bottom of the page. Use the lists on pages 30-31 as a reminder of whom to contact.

Checklist contacts

Local Press

Local radio stations

Local television

Whats on? hand-outs

Schools and colleges

Local charities and organisations

Local drama associations and their magazines

Keeping the campaign going!

Never forget your loyal supporters

An established good reputation for enjoyable productions is the best lever in the world with which to prise your audience out of their armchairs and into the local little theatre. Selling to those who already believe in you is the most important target of all, the backbone of the audience. It will yield more profitable returns than any other form of advertising.

It is more difficult, of course, for a new group to target the local audience. However, the novelty value of what is being planned and the natural curiosity of local friends and family will doubtless help to create your first audience and form the basis for a loyal audience of the future.

However, a new society might want to limit the number of performances accordingly to ensure reasonably full houses rather than half-empty ones. It is a simple matter to gradually increase the numbers of performances along with an established reputation and demand for tickets.

Keep records, mailing lists – and your audience

Do not lose this impetus. Always keep a record of who has attended a show. Individual members should all be encouraged to keep their own personal lists of their friends, relatives and colleagues who have been before and then to contact these people each time to remind them how much they enjoyed the show on the previous occasion. The society secretary or tickets sales personnel should send out advance information and booking forms to everyone in the group and to the regular supporters as well.

Build up a mailing list of members, patrons and regular supporters. Make sure advance booking forms go out to all these people – and reminders to follow on from these.

Maintaining audience numbers

If the production standards are as good as ever, there will be no trouble maintaining audiences and a hard core of solid support can gradually be added to as new members join and bring fresh contacts along as uninitiated audience members.

Never take all this for granted, however. Audiences need constant reminders and encouragement. It is a common mistake to assume that everyone will turn up as usual, particularly for the mid-week performances.

Name and Address	Contact	Telephone number	Other comments
The Echo 2 The Drive Anytown Post code or Zip code	Jane Somebody	0123 45678	Needs 2 weeks notice Send complimentary tickets

Selling even more tickets

Be consistent in both performance quality and in ticket-selling management. Keep up the standards and enthusiasm. Then, as the word spreads about how good the plays are, the circle of audience should sweep yet further.

Selling even more tickets

Be positive! A half-hearted approach to selling tickets will never work. Constantly maintain enthusiasm.

Groups and families

Encourage people to come in families and groups. It may be useful to offer a family night with reduced rates for several members of the family.

Local societies

Local societies often support each other. Arrangements can be made to visit each other's shows as party bookings on a reciprocal basis. The group will learn a lot about other plays, as well as how different societies and players work. Meanwhile, you will all have great evenings out and enjoy sharing your amateur theatre experiences.

You can also advertise in drama association magazines which link local groups' news together from your town or area.

Members' contribution

Set goals that members of the group should aim for, such as:

Selling the most tickets

Selling tickets to people who have never been to any of the society's productions before

Persuading a particular group to buy tickets this time

Selling to a group – say over eight or ten people

Having more than ten relatives come

A word or two of warning about advance sales

One of the problems with aggressive ticket selling early is extracting the money from advance sales. It can be difficult to persuade people to part with money until you have the actual tickets to hand over. Ideally ensure that the tickets are ready really early or, if this is not possible, issue an advance booking voucher that can be exchanged for tickets later.

Moreover, if you are trying to sell to a truly resistant person or group, they may agree to come just to 'keep the peace' – and then not turn up at all on the night. This can be galling if the seats were for a popular fully-booked night and so this action denies a real enthusiast the chance for a ticket.

Careful judgement is needed and a policy over which nights to promote hard – but often, once a ticket is sold and the new audience members do come along, they are surprised at the quality of local theatre. They may well become loyal regulars from that moment on.

Generally if people have actually handed over hard cash they are more likely to turn up than if they agree to 'pay on the door' or settle up with friends later. There is always the odd instance of a member of the group being left high and dry by friends who do not bother to show. This can be very annoying if the member has had to part with his or her own money to purchase the tickets on their behalf.

Timing and record keeping

As with all aspects of publicity, timing is all important. Advance booking should be made available to members of the society for a limited period with

---

ADVANCE BOOKING FORM FOR:

I wish to purchase   tickets for the performance on

day   date

I enclose a cheque for the amount of

Please make cheques payable to *

and send to

Name

Address

Telephone number (daytime)   Fax

Telephone number (evening)   Fax

Ticket prices and dates of performances *

(* Insert relevant information prior to despatch)

a deadline for the receipt of monies before the tickets 'go public'.

However the sales are handled, the ticket sales operative (who may be the Publicity Manager or part of the Front of House team or the Treasurer or somebody totally independent) will need to keep clear records of who has received advance tickets and on the exchange of monies for these.

In particular, exchanging sold tickets can lead to confusion if not very carefully controlled.

Tickets for sale. Apply within!

Local shops can generally be persuaded to sell tickets. Help them by providing clear information about dates and prices – and a safe container for the cash. And, in the politest possible way, try to ensure that all the members of the staff are aware of the ticket sales system so that no prospective audience members are turned away because only one particular sales person 'knows the ropes'.

When this happens, his or her absence, even for an hour, could forfeit valuable sales.

However willing a local trader is to help, ensure that their premises are open and manned at rational hours. If a single source of tickets always seems to be shut – or is open only at odd times, many potential purchasers will be frustrated and will probably decide against coming. Buying tickets must be easy.

On the streets

As a final reminder that the production is taking place, it is worth considering a procession through the streets in costume – perhaps on the weekend before the production. Suitably clad players (and/or their children) can seize this opportunity to hand out flyers and arouse local interest in the production. It takes courage and enthusiasm but once underway, especially if the weather is kind, can be quite stimulating and provides players with a taste of 'street theatre'.

To sum up . . .

1
A good publicity campaign needs to start early

2
Follow this first thrust with an equally energetic well-structured advertising campaign

3
Those involved should be positive and enthusiastic throughout

4
Your best customers are usually your old loyal ones

5
Do not miss any opportunity to reap extra audience from other quarters

6
Check out any specific type of audience member that will be interested in this particular production

7
Have a theme so that the printed matter all co-ordinates and suits the style of the production

8
Make sure posters are clear and informative

9
Make sure ticket sales are really well organised

10
Check all the checklists so that nothing and no-one is missed

Actors in costume publicise the production in the local vicinity

Count down

With the play well through the rehearsal stage, the cast and backstage team are fully aware of their various responsibilities and the final deadline of the opening night is just around the corner. Now is the time to make sure that everything that needs to be organised has indeed been allocated, taken care of, or is 'in hand'.

Most societies have an established management committee that will have allocated tasks to various willing members – but it is as well to double check that there have been no oversights or omissions before it is too late to remedy these.

Overall checklist for final stages

Front of House

Are enough people available to sort tickets and seating?

Are helpers available to sell programmes and raffle tickets?

Has a cash 'float' been organised?

Licenses and red tape

Is all the paperwork in order and the necessary licenses granted?

Have the authorities approved safety and fire precautions?

Is the insurance cover up to date?

Publicity

Are all the posters out?

Have flyers been distributed?

Have the Press and local television and radio been informed?

Do you know when reporters or photographers are expected?

Venue

Check the booking is still fine

Are there any complications to sort – unexpected or otherwise?

Have the seating plans been submitted to the relevant authorities?

Are there enough chairs for the anticipated audience?

Are tables, tablecloths, flowers and so on being organised?

Tickets and Box Office

How are the ticket sales progressing?

Have tickets been distributed to all the right people and points of sale?

Have all the advance booking forms been returned?

Properties and make-up

Check the lists to ensure everything is 'in house' or organised

Consult the stocklists and make sure no further supplies are needed

Raffle

Have sufficient prizes been contributed?

Have raffle tickets been bought?

Catering and Bar

Has a rota been established?

Are sufficient helpers available?

Are all the licences and health checks in order?

Have drinks and glasses been ordered?

Has a shopping list for food or refreshments been organised?

Who is going to buy and deliver the initial supplies?

Is there a system for topping up supplies?

Is there sufficient china and cutlery?

Overall checklist for final stages

Photography

Is someone set up to photograph rehearsals and performances?

Have arrangements been made for a video recording, if applicable (check copyright restrictions first)

Children

Are helpers organised to look after the youngsters?

Is there a suitable place for them to change and to be kept occupied backstage?

Stage management

Have sufficient stage hands been drafted in?

Does an intercom or monitor system need to be set up?

Are all the cue sheets organised?

Lighting, sound, sets and special effects

Is all the equipment in order and/or hiring of equipment in place?

If a lighting and/or sound tower is needed, is this organised?

Is any extra help needed to complete the set structure and painting?

Costumes

Are all the costumes ready?

Is extra help needed to complete sewing?

Is costume hire organised?

Is more help needed with costume changes backstage?

Venue

Organising the venue appropriately is very important. It must feel warm and welcoming so that the audience relax straight away. While the Front of House team need to ensure that sufficient numbers of helpers are available to greet the public with smiling faces as they assist them to find their seats, it is also important for a team of people to make sure in advance that the place will look and feel good. There are various ways to achieve this end, as the checklist below shows.

1

Try to ensure car parking is freely available

2

Put a banner above the outside door. Light this if possible

3

A main exterior light will make the venue more welcoming

4

Make sure the interior lighting is right, too – preferably not too glaring but certainly not gloomy

5

Make a display of photographs. These might be photographs of the present production, photographs of previous productions, 'portrait' photographs of the cast and directors, shots of the backstage team – or a mixture of them all!

Newspaper reports might also be included. This will take a while to organise so do not leave it entirely to the last minute.

You might also make a display advertising future productions

6

Check on the heating and the ventilation

Find out just how much this can be varied and adjusted to suit varying temperatures

7

Does anything need mending or washing beforehand? Nothing looks worse than torn drapes at the windows or smashed panes of glass, while doors that jam or creak can be very distracting, and may even be against safety regulations

Such problems are unlikely to be the actual responsibility of the theatre group but still need to be pointed out in good time to the venue organisers so that any necessary repairs or adjustments can be set in motion well before the first night. If the venue is available only at the last minute, checks on such matters must be a priority on first arrival.

8

Flower arrangements help to brighten up a dull hall

9

The flooring and carpeting needs to look respectable with no tears or other potential trip devices!

10

Is there a cloakroom? Are lottery type tickets needed to identify coats or articles deposited?

11

Is there a box office and does this need organising? What are the alternatives?

Final venue checks

Are all the fire exits and fire doors working and accessible?

Are fire extinguishers/hydrants in place? Check the weight to ensure that these are full.

Are the heaters and/or the air conditioning in good order?

Do the exit signs all light properly?

Is the emergency lighting working?

Are all the seats in the right place?

If appropriate, are the seats or tables numbered?

Do the seats need to be locked together?

Are the aisles wide enough?

Are the toilets clean?

Do any light bulbs need replacing?

Are sufficient rolls of toilet paper, soap and paper towels available? And where are extra stocks kept?

Do you know where all the tools and cleaning materials are kept in case of any spills or emergencies?

Is there a first-aid box?

Do you need *No Smoking* signs?

Are stairways well lit?

What access and facilities exist for the handicapped?

Are fire escapes working, accessible and safe?

What kind of ladders are available and where are these kept?

Can an intercom be set up to help communications from backstage to front of house and to the lighting and sound control areas?

Backstage checks

Backstage checks

Checks will also need to be made backstage to ensure that:

1

The make-up area is well lit and supplied with plenty of mirrors

2

The heating and the ventilation is all in order and can be adjusted to suit varying temperatures

3

There is room for the cast to change comfortably

4

There are plenty of hooks and hangers for clothes

5

An intercom is set up to help communications from frontstage to backstage and to the dressing rooms

6

There is clear access to the stage for stage hands when changing scenery

7

A convenient space is available to set out all the properties

8

Everything meets public health and fire regulations

9

Washing facilities are available and clean

10

Doors can be closed to isolate any extraneous sounds or noise backstage

11

There is sufficient storage to meet production requirements

During the final rehearsals, it can be difficult to find time to check everything so try to find time to analyse the state of the venue on a separate occasion in order to make sure that all is indeed 'up to scratch'. For example, you may need to ask the following questions:

Is the stage properly marked up for property positions?

Do the curtains run smoothly?

Are all the carpet edges down securely?

Does anything on stage need repairs or mending?

Does anything need washing?

Are the sightlines all being maintained?

Are all the steps safe?

Thursday 13 November

Remember to phone Nigel about mending the steps

Bring carpet tape and staple gun

Check spare light bulbs

Ring Tony to let him know the first heater is not working

Curtains— find a volunteer to stitch up drooping hem

Make lists. Do not ever rely upon your brain to remember everything

Front of House

Prior to the first night, the Front of House team will need to make sure that they are well organised, that every helper knows which performances they need to cover, what time they should arrive on duty and exactly what they will be expected to do. Responsibilities will vary from one society and venue to another, but generally the main aim is to ensure good relations with the audience, to welcome them, help them find their seats, to sell programmes and raffle tickets and generally to provide a smooth reception and good care of the public for the duration of the show.

Decide how many people are needed to do this comfortably and, if possible, have a few 'stand ins' lined up in case anyone is ill and/or you find that you need more bodies!

The venue checks listed may come under Front of House jurisdiction. Make sure everything is in good order before your audience arrives.

Front of House personnel will also be in charge of manning the box office, the seating arrangements, the setting out of tables and chairs and, possibly, organising the bar. All these tasks require a good deal of planning prior to the performances.

Bar

Selling drinks will boost the income from a show considerably, as well as providing a welcome service to a thirsty audience and helping them to relax. A bar may need to be set up, if this is not a permanent feature of the building. If this is the case, make sure you use a sturdy table so there are no wobbling glasses or bottles.

Front of house

If the theatre has it own bar, it is still wise to check that this will be available for the show and that bar staff are organised. If running your own bar, follow this procedure:

1

Check if the licence is in order

2

Organise a rota of reliable helpers who must, of course, be old enough to serve alcohol

3

Find somewhere safe to store cash

4

Organise a float

5

Order drinks. It may be useful to check the sales figures of previous shows to establish an estimate of what will be needed. Supplies for this kind of event are generally bought on a sale or return basis

6

You may need to organise hire of glasses

7

Decide who is going to transport the supplies and return any unused bottles – plus the glasses, if these have been hired

8

Establish a system for topping up supplies, should you have underestimated quantities or have insufficient space to store it all in one go

9

Make sure everything required for washing glasses is in house – you may need to supply tea-towels and washing-up liquid, for example

Organising a raffle

Raffles are great fund raisers and the audience usually enjoy the opportunity of trying to win a prize. There are really only a few things to organise beforehand, the most taxing of which is finding the prizes. If the company is in funds, they may simply buy a selection of suitable presents. Otherwise, the cast and backstage team can be asked to contribute – or local companies and stores may be willing to donate a few gifts. They can be thanked in the programme.

Make sure you have a sufficient supply of raffle tickets and enough people to tear up and fold these, once sold, in good time for the draw.

All that remains is to organise someone to do the draw which can take place in one of the intervals.

Seating

The audience may be seated in straight rows, around an 'apron stage', 'in the round' or at tables, cabaret style. Some venues have a fixed

A conventional seating arrangement has the stage at one end of the venue

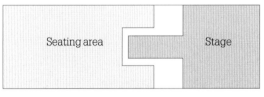

This is a thrust stage with a projecting apron

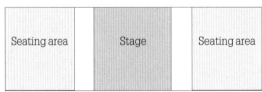

A centre stage is unusual. Actors need careful direction to ensure they perform to both seating areas

Here an open stage is surrounded on three sides by the audience

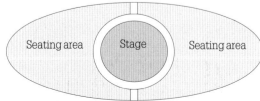

Theatre in the round places the actors in the centre core of their audience

arrangement so there are no options. Obviously the decision, if the audience is to be seated unconventionally, must be taken early on as all the elements of the production, especially the moves, will be radically affected.

Seating plans will have to be submitted to the local authorities for approval. Aisles must not be any narrower than a standard width in order to allow the venue to be cleared quickly in an emergency such as fire. For the same reason, emergency exits must be kept clear.

Moreover, apart from the safety factors, a good centre aisle makes it easier for the audience to reach their seats and for any usherettes, waiters and waitresses, and raffle or programme sellers to manoeuvre their way around

A good clear seating plan will also form the basis for the plan that keeps track of your ticket selling and which seats have been booked.

The audience capacity will also be subject to approval and will vary

according to the seating plan selected. For example, if very wide aisles are needed, the numbers will be reduced. In the same way, using tables will limit the numbers. So will maintaining the best possible visibility throughout the auditorium. Make sure that every member of the audience can see the action but that sightlines remain viable from all angles.

Different styles of play will work best with a different size of audience. If you are aware that the play you are doing will not sell in huge numbers, it can be

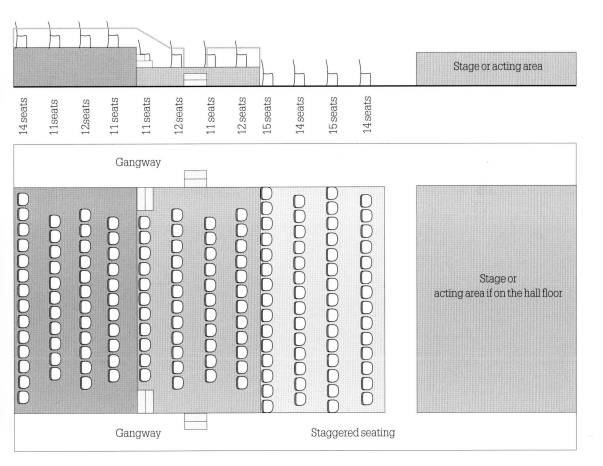

Raised and staggered seating means that every member of the audience should have a good view of the stage

Front of house, and catering

better to make the audience feel 'full' - by using wide aisles or manipulating the areas in some way so that the audience do not feel that they are rattling around in a vast space.

Using a wide transverse aisle in front of the stage or half way down the hall separating two separately priced sets of seats can work very well. The advantage then is that more rows of seats can be added if tickets suddenly sell much faster than expected.

The choice of chairs may not be in your control but try to ensure the seating is as comfortable as possible.

Seating around tables works very well for a cabaret, revue or pantomime. It is vital if food is to be served and does generally tend to create a convivial, friendly atmosphere.

Most people come to the theatre in pairs so it is best if rows contain even numbers of seats.

Bear in mind any other extraneous bodies that may be occupying space in the audience area. A pianist, small musical group or full orchestra may need to be accommodated. In certain productions, the cast may move among the audience or through the aisles. There may also be steps up to the stage as yet not in place. The prompt may be seated out front somewhere. Make sure there will still be sufficient space for your seating plan when all these elements have been taken into account and that there will be no compromise on the safety factors.

Ensure that both the row and seat numbers are very clear and firmly in place. Also that all the Front of House staff are familiar with the lay-out and numbering.

Box Office

> If the theatre has an established box office then all the necessary equipment will probably be in place. If you are starting from scratch, the following will be useful:
>
> Ticket racks or some secure place to hold unsold or reserved tickets
>
> Cash box
>
> Calculator
>
> The up-to-date plan of seating arrangements and tickets sold
>
> Pens, stationery, scissors, stapler and other office essentials
>
> Notebook
>
> Refuse bin
>
> If the society accepts credit cards then, obviously, a credit card machine will also be required

Many groups will be using a venue that serves multiple purposes and does not have an official box office. A table at the entrance may be all that is available. It is then even more important to be well organised and to use containers that prevent loose pens rolling away or tickets blowing off in a sudden draught.

Catering

It may be that outside caterers are going to supply your needs. If so, just make sure that they are booked well in advance, are fully aware of your requirements, and know where and when to come.

If doing your own catering, set up a rota of helpers to prepare food or refreshments, to serve these, to handle any cash, and to clear away afterwards.

Depending on the venue and local regulations, you may or may not be able to prepare food on the premises so check this out straight away. It may be necessary to make the food at home and then deliver this to the venue.

Tickets to be collected at the door need to be ready to hand out and easy to find. Keep them in alphabetical order – and if payment is due to be collected, make sure this is clearly stated

Catering

It is vital to ensure that the venue meets all the health regulations and that the food is good, fresh and prepared under hygienic conditions

1

Decide what is to be served or sold and then organise a shopping list for food or refreshments

2

Decide who is going to buy and deliver the initial supplies

3

Set up a system for topping up supplies, if this is needed, or to buy any fresh produce daily

4

Find out if the venue supplies china and cutlery. If so, is there sufficient? Sort out your own, if necessary – or make up any deficit. Everything must be scrupulously clean, of course

5

If food is being served at tables, these must be prepared beforehand. Clean tablecloths or disposable table 'runners' will be needed

6

Flowers help the tables look good – a small flowering pot plant on each table may survive better than flowers in a vase

7

Small night lights on a saucer provide sympathetic lighting on each table but may be against fire regulations. Ask your local fire officer for advice

8

Remember to buy napkins, refuse sacks, washing-up fluid and any other essentials

9

Check if you need to bring sponges or tea towels.

10

If ice creams are to be served, access to a refrigerator is an obvious need. Check this out

Ticket sales

Tickets may be sold in the following ways:

No seats allocated – first come, first served

Pre-booked individual seats

Pre-booked into a specific row but not a specific seat

Pre-booked tables

(see also pages 118-119)

As described on page 108 in the Publicity and printed matter section, pre-booking seats, rows or tables does encourage your audience to book earlier in order to procure the best seats and to ensure a group can sit together. There will be less of a free-for-all on the night. The down side is that the audience may arrive to take their seats a little later. If everyone arrives at the last minute, this may hold up the commencement of the show – and can cause considerable disturbance if the play has begun. None the less, selling pre-booked seats or a prebooked approximate location such as a table or row is the most professional approach. This is the way most societies work. It takes careful planning, however, and the establishment of a well-thought out system that will eliminate the risk of double-booking.

The following decisions have to be made about ticket prices:

How much is a conventional ticket going to cost?

Will different seats in the house command different prices?

Will matinée prices be different?

Will different nights carry a higher or lower price, depending on their popularity?

Will there be reduced rates for children, the elderly, the unemployed, and other such categories?

Will group bookings or school parties mean a reduced price

Will you offer special rates for families on a specific 'family' night?

Will you offer two seats for the price of one on certain nights?

How will you deal with any unsold tickets immediately prior to the performance? Will they be offered at a reduced rate?

Ticket sales

Booking seats plan

If individual seats are to be booked, you will need to prepare a seating plan for each performance and mark off the seats sold as the bookings are made. This can be complicated if tickets are being sold from several sources. In this case, a specific selection of seats will need to be allocated to each point of sale. This allocation can be adjusted later if necessary, to reflect the ebb and flow of sales from each place.

Codes can be used to indicate the type of ticket sold. For example, these codes might indicate if it is a ticket sold at a reduced rate for a child, a group booking, a complimentary ticket for patrons or the press, and so on. Letters can be used, as follows:

A = Adult

C = Child

F = Free/complimentary

G = Group

and so on

Or you might devise a system of colour coding, colouring in the seats with felt tip pens.

The main thing is to be consistent, to be sure everyone knows exactly what to do and to keep the system as simple as possible.

If a local store is selling tickets on a voluntary basis, they may not wish to undertake a complicated booking system and since you will be grateful for their help and know that they are undoubtedly very busy people, you will need to compromise. If they prefer to simply jot down notes, it will then be up to a member of the group to update the records and master seat plan on a daily basis in order to relieve

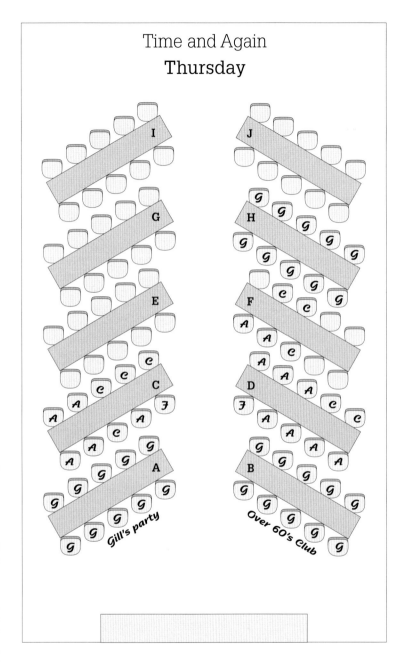

Time and Again
Thursday

Gill's party

Over 60's Club

Once a booking is confirmed and paid for, mark the seat on the plan with an appropriate code or colour. When tables are used, a group will often book an entire table

A - Adult

C - Child

F - Free or complimentary

G - Group

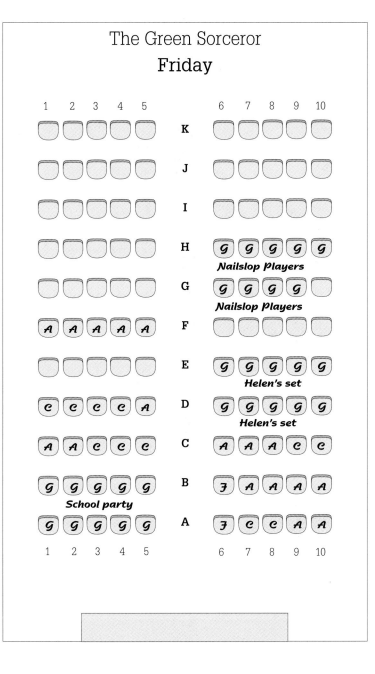

The Green Sorceror
Friday

your ticket sellers of any extra work. In any case, regular checking may avoid errors and confusion.

It is important to use a different way of marking the seats if the booking is only provisional and not to score out any seat allocation entirely until monies have exchanged hands.

Make sure that all points of sale are provided with a float and a secure cash box.

To sum up . . .

The opening night approaches. On stage, the producer and cast will be rehearsing furiously now to meet this deadline, with pep-talks and reminders to keep the momentum going.

As the final dress rehearsal ends, it will be time to look forward to having an audience at last. The backstage teams, too, will have been fine tuning all their various departments' hard work and adding the final touches to sets, costumes and so on.

Your vigorous publicity campaign and press reports should have ensured that lots of tickets have been sold.

Meanwhile, if all the checklists in this chapter have been ticked off, then the venue and front of house team will be ready to greet the public and welcome them to another stunning production by a well-organised group.

The blank plan will need to be duplicated for each performance. It might be colour coded to match the tickets.

Always check if patrons. the press, or someone who has made a valuable contribution to the production is to be given complimentary tickets

The Show

Start with enthusiasm!

Start with energy!

Front and backstage should be humming with activity and excitement, with the inevitable first-night nerves lending a vibration, a timbre to the music of the 'overture' of everybody warming up. The audience, too, will be full of anticipation now, waiting to see what the evening's entertainment will present to them.

The producer's main task is over. Now, in performance, it will be up to the cast, the stage manager and the backstage team to keep the show flowing. In the auditorium, the front of house team will be 'performing' too, acting as hosts and hostesses to the arriving audience.

The audience has their part to play, too. They are an integral element of the production. Like a vital member of the cast who has not yet been to a rehearsal, their contribution will lift the show into another league and complete the jigsaw puzzle.

The producer and the cast

While the producers retire to take a back seat at this stage, the cast will, none the less, be acutely aware of the producer's reactions and will want to please them and earn their approval in performance.

It is important that the cast feel happy and keen, ready to start with gusto. Although there will be a few 'butterflies in tummies', the exhilaration of receiving an audience response at last will soon overcome these, so long

as all the cast are confident of reasonable success. If they have rehearsed thoroughly, have learned their lines well in advance and know that they can rely on each other and that they have the support of a good backstage team – then those first nerves will soon disappear, leaving an edge of excitement that can make for a really fine performance.

There is no excuse for a poor first-night show. There may indeed be the odd technical hiccup with a new or untried piece of equipment whose contrariness slipped through the net in the technical run-through but the well-rehearsed group should take any minor mishaps in their stride and, if the odd line is lost or mutates through first-night stage fright, this will not matter a jot – so long as the pace is maintained.

Avoid overcrowded wing areas

An interest in the audience response and sudden nervousness over missing their entrances may lead to an influx of extra bodies in the wings. Ideally, the stage manager can call or send for actors when they are needed to prevent their arriving unnecessarily early, while monitors or intercoms will allow those backstage to keep track of what is happening on stage.

Enjoying the laughter

Audience response is wonderful . . . but it is a new ingredient and can be handled well or badly, especially laughter. The timing is all-important. The actors should learn to 'play with' the laughter, coming in with the next line just as the crescendo is topped and begins to crest – like a wave breaking. The laughter will drown vital lines if the actors gabble on regardless. Moreover, the audience

1
Remind the cast of sightlines

2
Dissuade the cast from hovering in the wings to watch, tripping up stage hands and generally getting in the way

3
Install an intercom to the dressing room so that the cast can hear the play. This will help enormously. (If a camera can be set out front and linked to a monitor backstage, this is even better!) With or without such aids, however, the cast need to have been drilled to keep track of the play's timing and their entrances

4
No-one has an excuse for missing their cue – or turning up far too early and obstructing others – if they have concentrated properly during rehearsals

5
If children are involved, they need to be told that peering through the curtains to see if their relatives have turned up is not to be tolerated.

It looks awful out front, and if one child starts, soon all the other youngsters will join in. Then the backstage team setting the stage will have to battle with a heaving mass of bodies, giggling and scrambling for a viewpoint will be unable to relax and laugh properly if their response is cut off too abruptly. They will instinctively start to 'prune' their laughter themselves in order to hear the play. This is the last thing you want to happen.

Laughter can occur at the most unexpected times. Aside from those humorous moments you had not anticipated in a comedy, straight plays can also evoke laughter. In a thriller, especially, it can be very unnerving for those on stage when laughter breaks out in a highly dramatic scene. This, in fact, is quite common. It is a normal human reaction to giggle when nervous, just as schoolchildren do when a teacher is angry. It is a release mechanism. So a tense audience will often start to laugh. Be prepared for this.

Cast and crew

As well as the actors, the backstage team – lights, sound, wardrobe, props and all – will welcome a note of encouragement and support from the producer or director before curtain up. They will all be very busy immediately beforehand, checking properties, equipment and so on – so do not linger. A brief, cheery word is all that is required.

Maintaining concentration backstage

Both the actors and backstage team must concentrate on what is happening – on and off stage. Relaxing too much in the changing room, sharing a joke and indulging in a glass of beer, will be at their peril if they forget how soon their entrances or specific responsibilities are due. Producers should remind the cast and crew that the pace is always different with an audience – plus the fact that there is

always the risk that the cast might skip a few lines, or pages even, and thus alter the timing dramatically. Everyone must listen to the intercom or note the ebb and flow of the actors' entrances and exits.

Drinking to calm the nerves can have a dire effect if taken to excess – especially as the adrenaline will be flowing well already. Most people feel on a real high during a successful opening night – without any alcohol to boost the glow of triumph. A good first performance is very exciting and can be achieved best by a sober cast!

Awareness of relatives out front, especially partners and parents, can add to the tension and there may be a resurrection of the first-night nerves for individual performers later in the week, as and when this occurs. Others rise to the occasion and revel in the opportunity to 'show off' to somebody they know out front! So, if there is any unexpected change in the level of a performance – one way or the other – it may be that the presence of a relative is to blame!

Team spirit

Just how the team pulls together and supports each participant is very important. Both actors and the backstage workers' contributions are now being put to the test too. Indeed, the actors' performances depend on the support of the backstage team, who will be feeling nervous and excited just like those out front.

Producer's role

A good luck card from the producer to the cast and to the back-stage team will be welcomed, as will a brief personal appearance backstage to wish them all the best before the show

Basically, on and off the stage, the following applies:

1

Everyone should consider everyone else's feelings and needs as generously as possible and rally to the cause of making the show work well

2

The production will benefit greatly from co-operation within the ranks!. The actors must help each other if things go wrong. They should also help each other when things go well – in order to maximise the success

3

Personal pride should be manipulated to contribute to the well-being of the team, rather than being pursued for its own selfish ends. It is, in any case, a good feeling to revel in the warmth of a family-like group that works closely together and shares a common goal

begins. Producers should resist any urge to nag over minute details as everyone will be highly strung now. Just tell them all that they have the makings of a great show and ask them to do their best. Then retire to watch.

It can be very unsettling for the producer to be standing out front, suddenly cut off – unable to intervene or contribute. Instead the producer feels nervous for everyone and everything. While actors and back-stage team tend to worry most about their own individual appearances and

The opening night: a good send-off

Dealing with any problem areas

In an imperfect world, there are bound to be a few hiccups. If there are problems . . .

1

The producer should not inflict any sweeping changes on the team now – unless the situation is really desperate. Drastic changes, without the opportunity to rehearse these properly with all concerned, will throw everybody and are likely to make the problems worse, rather than better

2

However, prior to the next performance the producer should, clearly and tactfully, suggest how those improvements that are really essential can be achieved

3

Bear in mind that everyone's egos cry out to be pampered right now, not crushed, and that self confidence and tempers are particularly fragile at this first-night stage

4

Do not spoil the opening night by making unnecessary deprecating remarks. Most offenders will be only too well aware if they have 'let the side down' in any way and will be found profusely apologising for a late entrance or a missed cue, or a prop left in the wrong place

5

Be supportive and sympathetic, not acidly critical. Point out any problem areas that must be addressed but do so with humour and constructive help

6

It can be difficult to catch everybody backstage with any little comments as they are likely to be scattered and rushing about so if the producer thinks some extra reminders are necessary, it is a good idea to pin up a notice somewhere prominent

---

responsibilities, the producer frets about every aspect of the production and is aware of each minute detail, good and bad.

The other side of this coin is that, just like the anxieties, the exhilaration in a good production is also multiplied out for the producer. This myriad cluster of nerves and pleasure, relief and sheer joy when a great show takes off can be quite overwhelming – and very exciting if the play fulfils or surpasses expectations!

The producer will have some last-minute reminders for both the cast and the backstage teams. Pinning up a notice ensures that everyone 'gets the message'

Break a leg, everyone!
Let's make this a great show.

Remember to:
Keep up the pace
Be fast on cues and entrances
Smile!
Keep the noise level down backstage.

There is a party at my place on Thursday night, after the show. You are all very welcome . . . please bring a bottle or two.

There is a great write-up in The Gazette - Ron has copies for you all.

Fiona sends her best wishes to you and hopes the play will be a great success; she says she'll bring the baby along to meet you all at the next show.

Now go and 'sock it to them'! Keep them laughing!

Gill X X X X X X X

The second and succeeding nights

A successful first night is very exhilarating – but also exhausting. All that adrenaline and nervous energy will take its toll, not to mention any post-play celebrations that might have crept into the early hours and involved a certain intake of alcohol! But there are further performances still to come – which it is hoped will be equally good, if not better. Every audience deserves the best!

Pace

Generally, as the play rolls, first-night nerves are left behind, the routine becomes more familiar and the play should speed up. However, especially on the second night, there is often a feeling of anti-climax and the pace can, in fact, slacken. Actors are heard hotly protesting that the audience is poor: 'They are not nearly so responsive as last night.'

Audiences do vary: some will be better than others and laugh or cry more readily. Saturday night audiences, and those with group bookings who create their own party atmosphere, are usually good. However, often it is the cast who are themselves to blame when an audience is less responsive than they hope. After the first-night high the players are more tired and the initial launch excitement is over. So, if the audience fail to laugh at that first great joke or gasp when the murder weapon is drawn – the cast may feel let down and, discouraged – and can fail to give of their very best.

In fact, if an audience seems a little difficult, it is up to the players to take up the challenge and to work that much harder. The cast should never allow themselves to drift into a half-hearted performance.

This is where the producer may need to march backstage and jolly everyone into a more positive approach. The cast must be urged to keep up the pace. The producer will have been closely watching the reactions and facial expressions out front and can probably reassure the cast that the audience are, in fact, enjoying the show. Yes, they may need to unwind a little more – the interval will help this process. Meanwhile, the cast must keep up the highest standards. An audience must be wooed and won. Never allow a quiet audience to slow the play's pace, to drag the actors down. Instead make sure the cast see this as a challenge and that everyone gives the play the most vigorous attack possible. When a slow audience is turned around into an obviously appreciative one, this is especially gratifying.

Final night speeches: to give or not to give . . .

At the end of the performance, do not inflict long speeches on an audience. These will detract horribly from the final flourish. It does not happen in the professional theatre, and can be a real bore for the audience who are usually not the slightest bit interested in votes of thanks.

If it is impossible to avoid, if tradition dictates that you must give the producer flowers or champagne publicly on the last night, make it brief – and part of the flow, if possible. Like every other part of the production, such a presentation needs to be well thought through and as properly rehearsed as it can be, bearing in mind that such gifts are meant to be a surprise!

If the play is a musical, revue or other such light entertainment, try to insert this brief tribute before the final resounding encore so that the show still finishes on a high.

Of course, if the play is a serious one then the final curtain call must be completed first. Most especially if the production is a highly dramatic or tragic play, then to rush straight into a sudden gushing of thanks and laughter straight afterwards can be very inappropriate. So, if you feel strongly that the presentation will detract from the play's ending, stick to your guns and insist that the tributes must be saved for a private party afterwards.

Stage management

The Stage Manager is now in charge. It is his or her responsibility to keep the show rolling unless there is an emergency such as a fire – in which case he or she will be in control of organising a smooth exodus of the cast and backstage crew.

Meanwhile the Front of House team will organise the audience's exit!

Hopefully there will be no such disasters! The play will flow smoothly from start to finish. Everything will have been so well organised beforehand and so well practised during the final rehearsals that running the production will be a thoroughly enjoyable experience.

The lists below and on page 53 clarify exactly what must be done, although levels of responsibility do vary from group to group.

Production timing and intervals

Ideally, the Stage Manager will already have timed the run of the show during the dress rehearsals. It is of enormous help to everyone to keep track of what happens when – and how much time is available before a cue is due. If, for example, a smoke machine needs to be turned on to warm up for a minimum amount of time prior to its use, then this can be organised more efficiently. If a runner

Running the show

1
Turn up in plenty of time so that the last-minute checks are not done in a state of panic

2
Check everyone has arrived. Have a register and tick off arrivals – check the cast and the backstage team. If you have not organised a register, then keep a copy of the programme specifically for this purpose. It should serve as a list of who is expected to turn up front and backstage

3
Make a final check of the stage set and properties. Is everything ready for the succeeding scenes?

4
Are all the marked up scripts and/or cue sheets set out ready?

5
Are all the communication systems working properly, whether intercoms, telephones, monitors or whatever? Are you properly in touch with all the backstage team, the dressing rooms and Front of House?

6
Pin up any notices or items of interest. These might be final thoughts from the producer, press notices, Good Luck cards or party invitations

7
As the time for curtain up approaches, the stage manager will need to give everyone a reminder of the timing, whether 'Five minutes, please!' or whatever is appropriate. Then, before the show begins – and after each interval, prior to curtain up on the next act – always check whether:

A
The stage is set for the right scene

B
The props are all in the correct places

C
The beginners are changed, made up and ready

D
All the technicians are ready to start

E
Any special effects are organised

F
The prompt is in place with the right script

G
The musicians are ready

H
Any fast-change organisation is in hand

I
The audience are, for the most part, settled down in their seats

8
At the end of the show, the stage manager and assistants should take time to tidy up, put everything back in order and to set the stage ready for the opening scene the next night

Then if any item is missing, broken or whatever, they will have a whole day to organise whatever needs to be done. It also makes the start of the next performance less fraught

9
Always remember to thank all the stage hands for their hard work

needs to be sent to collect children from another venue for their entrance, or if an actor wants to know if there is time nip back home and fetch a forgotten item, then the Stage Manager knows precisely how long is available. An awareness of this lends greater control. For instance, interval times may be shortened if the Stage Manager can see that the play is running too long.

Obviously, the timing will alter with an audience. Laughter, or any form of audience participation, may lengthen the run but, at the same time, the pace will probably pick up with repeated performances. So make sure the chart includes new columns into which you can insert these adjusted timings for every performance.

1	*Strike final scene*
2	*Vacuum stage*
3	*Set first scene*
4	*Check smoke machine unplugged and adequate supply left for tomorrow*
5	*Check cave 'drop' ready for scene 2*
6	*Put wind machine in place*
7	*Refill snow bag*
8	*Close stage curtains*
9	*Check exit lights all still working*
10	*Check props room locked*
11	*Check all fine with FOH*
12	*Lock hall and return key to Alan*

Typical Stage Manager's post-performance list and play timing

Play timing

ACT 1	1st Dress rehearsal	2nd Dress rehearsal	Wed	Thurs	Fri	Sat
Scene 1						*↓Later start*
start	2.30	7.45	7.30	7.30	7.30	7.35
end	2.50	8.04	7.48	7.47	7.48	7.54
Scene 2						
start	2.52	8.07	7.50	7.48	7.49	7.55
end	3.10	8.23	8.05	8.04	8.03	8.10
NB Children needed mid-scene						
Scene 3						
start	3.15	8.25	8.07	8.05	8.04	8.11
end	3.30	8.38	8.20	8.18	8.16	
Scene 4						
start	3.38	8.40	8.21	8.19	8.17	8.26
end	4.15	9.00	8.40	8.37	8.36	8.44
Act 1 Total time	1 hr 45	1 hr 15	1 hr 10	1 hr 07	1 hr 06	1 hr 09
INTERVAL						
start	4.15	9.00	8.40	8.37	8.36	8.44
end	4.45	9.20	9.00	8.54	8.56	9.09
	(30 m)	(20 m)	(20 m)	(17 m)	(20 m)	(25 m)

ACT 2	1st Dress rehearsal	2nd Dress rehearsal	Wed	Thurs	Fri	Sat
Scene 1						
start	4.45	9.20	9.00	8.54	8.56	9.09
end	5.05	9.40	9.18	9.12	9.14	9.26
Scene 2						
start	5.07	9.42	9.20	9.13	9.15	9.27
end	5.19	9.53	9.31	9.25	9.27	9.38
Scene 3						
start	5.24	9.57	9.33	9.27	9.29	9.39
end	5.34	10.07	9.43	9.38	9.40	9.50
Scene 4						
start	5.36	10.08	9.45	9.39	9.41	9.51
end	5.55	10.25	10.00	9.55	9.58	10.08
Scene 5						
start	6.01	10.29	10.02	9.56	10.00	10.09
end	6.18	10.45	10.16	10.10	10.14	10.24
Act 2 Total time	1hr 33	1 hr 25	1 hr 16	1hr 16	1 hr 18	1 hr 15
Total run + interval	3 hrs 48	3 hrs	2 hr 46	2 hr 40	2 hr 44	2 hr 49
Audience gone by			10.30	10.25	10.27	10.45

↓interval 5 mins longer

Front of house

Front of house

The Front of House staff now have a vital role to play. They are the ambassadors of the society. Having organised themselves well ahead (see page 46), they will be ready to greet the public with confident, smiling faces. First impressions are very important so, even if there are any hiccups, it is vital to remain charming and unflustered.

With everything double-checked and in order, the doors can now be opened to the public.

Prior to curtain-up and towards the end of intervals, warning bells or an announcement will help direct the audience to take their seats.

Customer liaison: keeping the audience happy

House checks

There are certain procedures and checks that need to be made prior to the audience's arrival:

1
Check all the house lights, exit lights and emergency lights are working

2
Unlock security chains and bolts from exits

3
Is the stage curtain closed?

4
Check that the auditorium is clean and tidy

5
Make sure the float is sufficient and ready

6
Prepare any reserved tickets for collection

7
Check if there are enough programmes to sell

8
Put out raffle prizes and tickets

9
Put up a sign showing approximate time of the final curtain

10
Check photograph display is all in order (see chart on page 122)

11
If tables are being used, are the cloths clean and flowers in place?

12
Are all the seats set out correctly?

13
Are torches all working properly?

14
If a cloakroom is being provided, are the right personnel ready with their cloakroom tickets to hand?

Front of House

Trouble-shooting

1
Someone is sitting in the wrong seats

2
Customers claim they have already paid for those tickets being held at the door, but there is no record of this

3
The customers are holding tickets for a different night's performance

4
There has been an administrative 'cock-up' resulting in a double booking

5
The audience move their seats about, blocking aisles and exits

6
Customers complain that they cannot see properly

7
For some reason, there do not seem to be sufficient seats

8
You run out of loose change

9
Certain members of the audience are talking loudly during the show

It is relatively easy to keep happy customers smiling. The role of customer liaison becomes more difficult to fulfil well, when problems arise.

Whatever, the difficulties, the most important thing is to remain calm and confident. If you become flustered, then stress levels will rise rapidly all around you.

Front of House guidelines

1
Be sympathetic, and helpful – but firm

2
Deal with the problems promptly

3
Try to get everyone seated as quickly as possible

4
Make sure there are sufficient helpers available to be able to relay messages to others concerned and to keep queues to a minimum

5
Be very polite when you are asking people to move their seats or to be quiet

6
Apologise profusely if any fault lies with the society and work a few miracles to resolve the situation in whatever way you can

7
Make sure a few spare chairs are available for emergencies and that there are places for them that will not in any way infringe safety and fire regulations

8
A telephone, mobile or otherwise, may speed up the sorting out of problems

Meanwhile, those selling the programmes and raffle tickets need to be enthusiastic, efficient and well organised in order to deal with the flow of people quickly.

The entire Front of House team should remain alert to any further problems arising throughout the production. They may need to act quickly if someone is taken ill, for example. Specialist organisations and local rescue squads, such as the Red Cross or St John's Ambulance (in the UK) may be able to offer volunteers to be on hand for such emergencies.

The show begins

When the audience have all arrived and been seated, it will be the House Manager's responsibility to let the Stage Manager know that everything is fine out front and that the show can start. Late arrivals may cause a disturbance; if people are still flowing in, it may be better to delay the curtain opening for a few more moments.

Then, during the show, the House Manager will have to ensure that everything is in hand for the interval. If there are specific catering staff, it is wise to check with them that everything is ready and draft in extra help if there are problems. If Front of House are themselves providing beverages and refreshments then, with the audience settled, some house staff will need to divert their energies in this direction. Meanwhile the House Manager should note down any requirements for the next performance – such as extra raffle tickets or fresh flowers for the tables.

During the last act, the Front of House team will need to 'cash up' and check that that all the sales figures for the evening are properly recorded.

Post-performance

Final tasks after the show

1
Say good-bye to the audience cheerfully and make note of any good comments to pass on to all concerned

2
Secure the cash

3
Tidy up

4
Check your notes to see if anything has to be bought or sorted for the next night

5
Make sure everything is switched off, there are no taps running and no fire risks from abandoned cigarettes

6
Then, finally, fix safety chains, lock up and/or hand over keys to whomsoever is responsible for these

Cash flow and control

Each Front of House department should keep a clear record of their specific takings for every performance. As well as being vital documentation for the current production and the accounts, this will be a very useful record for future reference and anticipating the kind of levels of income that each element raises.

It can help future planning if ticket sales on the door are recorded independently of any settling up for reserved seats. So, each night, separate records should be noted for:

Catering and the bar

Box office – reserved seat payment

Ticket sales on the door

Meals

Refreshments

Bar

Raffle

Programmes

A final total for each of these aspects can then be recorded after the final performance.

Catering and the bar

As with any catering operation, most of the difficult preparation will have been undertaken prior to the arrival of the audience. So now the main tasks are the sale or presentation of the meal or refreshments, ensuring the audience can eat and drink well, that they are served politely – and then to tidy up afterwards.

If the ticket is an all-inclusive one, then extra monies may not need to be exchanged for the food, but alcoholic drinks will generally involve payment so, once again, a cash box of some kind, a float and a calculator perhaps, will keep life simple.

As with all the Front of House staff, the bar staff, waiters and waitresses need to be smiling and welcoming, efficient, courteous, able to serve quickly and to keep a clear head – especially in the interval rush.

It may help to have a ticket system whereby specific coloured tickets can be purchased in advance and then exchanged for goods of a certain value. This will ease the panic during the interval. Or drinks may be ordered and paid for in advance – to be exchanged later for a cloakroom style ticket. Alternatively, if there is room, simply set out the drinks ready with the appropriate tickets for the customers to retrieve themselves.

Plenty of refuse sacks will be needed for a swift tidy up if food has been served. Manoeuvring amongst an audience can be difficult and those serving and clearing away will need to have quick reactions and be good at balancing acts!

If the production is cabaret style, then drinks and refreshments may be served by waiters and waitresses throughout the evening. They will need to move quietly and unobtrusively – and to carry copious amounts of change in their apron pockets!

Cast and backstage tabs

If the cast and backstage crew are purchasing drinks or refreshments, it is useful to set up a tab in order to keep account of monies owing.

Someone responsible needs to be in charge and it is, of course, vital to catch all the debtors before they vanish after the play!

Videos and photographs

Every play deserves to be recorded properly. It is important to organise this well in advance and to use skilled photographers whenever possible.

See page 25 for information on video copyright.

Tips for taking still shots and videos

1
Watch the entire play through first to understand the flow and to know which moments or facial expressions will be the most interesting to focus upon

2
Check all the equipment beforehand to make sure everything is in working order

3
Ensure a good mix of close-ups and distant shots

4
Try to achieve a variety of eye levels and angles. Sit, stand, crouch. Climb up on a safe chair or table. Shoot from the right of the stage, from the left, and centre onto the stage

5
Do not concentrate only on the principals. Look out for interesting little gems on the 'sidelines', too

As a pictorial record of the play, copies of photographs will be appreciated by both the cast and crew while the main set will form part of the society's archive

Tips for taking still photographs

1
Check you have sufficient films and batteries

2
Take shots of the sets during final rehearsals: these will be very useful for future reference

3
Stage lighting can be good enough to allow the use of high-speed film without flash; this can produce excellent 'moody' results

4
Make sure every member of the cast is included!

5
Take plenty of shots; don't be mean!

6
Take back-stage shots as well as photographs of the play in action

Tips for making good videos

1
Move around: make sure the play is shot from lots of different angles to add interest. A fixed position video throughout can mean a very static result

2
Film several performances of the play in order to be able to edit together the best possible result

3
Ensure that the microphones are set to pick up the performers' voices rather than audience noise

4
Record the title, year and date as part of the film

5
Make sure batteries are properly charged or that fresh ones are available

To sum up . . .

The play is now an event. It is not just an idea, a vision, in the director or producer's mind; it is not just the way the actors and directors have worked things out in rehearsal; it is not just the practical application of all those techniques like lighting and sound.

It is an entity in its own right. It is a theatre experience for both the performers and the audience. All at once, it has become a part of the society's 'portfolio'.

This has been made possible because of a good deal of hard work and organisation. But this is not over yet. Even as the play's final performance draws to a close, and the backstage team move in to strike the last set piece, the organisation and team work continues – there will be quite a lot to do in order to 'wrap up' this show and to prepare for the next.

Aftermath

Although the actual performances are complete, there are still many things to do and still a good deal of pleasure to be had from sharing the company of those involved – and, in due course, from the memories of the show. As ever, practical tasks must be allocated in order to tidy up all the loose ends. The sets do not carry themselves off the stage. The costumes do not leap into the laundry or the lights run back down the road to the hire company – and the memory bank will be better served if there are photographs and videos to stimulate recollections.

Last-night party

Most societies like to celebrate after the final performance, to 'see off' the show in style. A party after the play – with music, food and wine – seals the success and is a great opportunity for both the active members of the group and their relatives and friends to mingle, to discuss the play and to plan for the future.

The social aspect of any dramatic society or group is a vital element of the whole. Enjoying convivial activities helps to bind the group together – and the fun of such events will be part of the attraction to new members who come along.

Party pieces – especially songs and odes about the production – often form the highlight of a post-play party and provide the chance to express

> Even if there is no 'cabaret', usually there will need to be some announcements made. Generally, you will need to include the following:
>
> **1**
> Thanks to everyone involved
>
> **2**
> Call to help with the clearing up – state times
>
> **3**
> Some information about the next production and dates of the first readings or auditions
>
> **4**
> A reminder about any items that must be returned to the society, or, on behalf of the society, to a third party or hire company

thanks and gratitude in an informal and entertaining way.

New recruits

Party cabaret pieces provide a good opportunity for the backstage team and young offspring to have a go on stage, too. Hidden talents of all kinds may be revealed!

Moreover, parties – and any other such post-performance gatherings throughout the run – are an excellent time to talk to friends who have enjoyed the show to see if there are any possible new recruits. The enjoyment of an excellent evening's entertainment generally makes people more receptive to the possibilities of taking part in the future, either front or backstage. So 'strike while the iron is hot!'

Names and addresses

Initial enthusiasm will soon pall if interest is not fanned by a prompt and enthusiastic follow-up. Always note down somewhere permanent the names and telephone numbers of any interested parties and be sure to contact them again very soon with any dates or relevant information.

HELP!
Clearing up starts at 10am on Sunday. Please come and help

Have you remembered to return all costumes – return all props – pay your bar tab?

Using fun clip art gives some important notices more impact

THE RED CARPET
Auditions
3, 7, 10 September
Everyone welcome

Clearing up

The anticlimax

Once the last night is over, all the exhilaration and the glow of triumph can be followed by a sudden 'low'. The frantic preparations that have culminated in performance and the fun of audience response have now peaked and, although it is often a relief that the pressure is less, it is also likely that many members will miss the excitement and camaraderie and will be heard complaining, 'Next week is going to seem really boring!'

Spreading the load

Now it is time to clear away the debris and to think about the next production. The more members that turn up, the easier the tidying up will be – and, because the work-load is then less burdensome, the more likely it will be that there will be a good turn-out next time too.

If, on the other hand, only a few arrive to help, the task will take that much longer and prove far more onerous. As grumbles, grouses, and sanctimonious comments fly, the sense of team spirit will soon be undermined.

So try to ensure solid support – and make the work as much fun as possible. It can be very satisfying to see the venue swiftly transformed from chaos into order again.

A lunch somewhere afterwards might even be organised so the event becomes a social one too.

Retaining the family feeling

Every play creates its own individual 'family' of cast and backstage members whose linked talents, energies and enthusiasms have welded into a close-knit group for the duration of the production. Even as the debris is being swept away, already the anecdotes about this particular show are being absorbed into the folklore of the society, to be drawn upon in later years, to regale new members with, 'Of course this was before your time, but there was once this hilarious situation when . . . .'

There is always a sadness about parting company from good friends. As the players gather to sweep up, to tidy, to collect their personal belongings, each one is aware that now is the last time this particular set of people will be closely involved in this particular play. There will be changes next time and, as the set is taken down, there is a funereal feel about the end of it all. It can seem almost sacrilegious to discuss the next set or the next costumes when this play is still not quite buried!

While the impact of this production remains absolutely fresh, compliments are shared and exchanged along with the sweeping brushes and refuse bags! 'Everyone says it's definitely the best we've ever done.'

Sometimes there are even tears – and the exchange of telephone numbers and signatures on programmes marks a desperate attempt to keep the unit intact as the last shreds of paper and polystyrene, cans, crisps, cotton-wool balls flushed with face powder, scrumpled tissues and programmes are swept away.

On the more formal side, it is useful if the society secretary, or somebody official, makes sure that all relevant addresses and telephone numbers have been duly recorded, especially of new recruits or possible patrons – and all debts (whether for ticket sales or the bar tab) are settled or noted!

Checklist

Venue

Much depends on the hire arrangements and who is responsible for re-establishing the status quo of the venue but generally you will need to:

Open the windows for fresh air!

Tidy box office, auditorium and all backstage areas

Check toilets and cloakrooms

Clear away refuse and organise removal of this if necessary

Wash up

Remove or rearrange tables and seating as applicable

Return any borrowed tables and chairs

Generally sweep, tidy, and vacuum

Clean surfaces in kitchen areas

Gather together any abandoned items or 'lost property'

Make-up

Tidy up make-up room

Store make-up carefully

Note any items that need replacing or 'topping up'

Return any hired wigs

Clearing up and de-briefing

Properties

Check the stage and dressing rooms for any scattered properties

Gather everything together and check nothing is missing from property lists

Store permanent props

Return immediately any props that belong to members present at the clear-up

Arrange for the return of others as applicable

Catering and bar

Clear away the debris

Wash glasses, cutlery and crockery

Arrange for return of glasses and any sale or return items

Launder any items such as tablecloths or tea towels

Costumes

Gather the costumes all together

Check nothing is missing from costume lists

Separate out hired or borrowed costumes ready for return

Launder own costumes as necessary

Make any repairs

Store costumes carefully

Lighting, sound, special effects

Derig the lights and safety chains, sound equipment and any special effect items

Store away the society equipment carefully

Return hired or borrowed equipment as soon as possible

Note any blown bulbs or other technical problems for future reference

Check if any replacements are needed

Check that all the venue's electrics have been left in a safe condition

Tidy control booth

Take down any temporary scaffolding or lighting towers

Sets

Strike set

Store flats and any other permanent features

Arrange for the disposal of temporary structures

Store carefully any useful paints or materials

Store society tools and return borrowed items

De-briefing

The hall is finally tidy. Vehicles overflow with boxes and bags of costumes, abandoned scripts, lighting equipment, properties, hired equipment and sundry lost properties. Now there may be time for a last impromptu gathering. This may take place over coffee at the hall or the members may drift across to the local public house. Members may even, as suggested earlier, meet together for lunch. Everyone then has a chance to discuss the high points of this show while the seeds of enthusiasm can be sown for the next production.

Such a gathering is very useful and due note should be taken of relevant comments. Never the less, this informal post mortem should be succeeded in due course by a formal society meeting to discuss the play's success or otherwise and to plan for the future accordingly.

It will be appropriate to discuss both the good and the bad points of the production, to analyse these so that the group can learn from its mistakes and build on the foundation of its strengths. Make lists of these strengths and weaknesses and adjust future plans, bearing in mind the good points, any areas marked for attention and suggestions as to how any improvements might be achieved.

Assess the following:

Script

Auditions and casting

Line-learning

Cast reliability

Rehearsals and schedule

Sets and stage hands

Lighting, sound, special effects

Costumes

Properties

Music

De-briefing

Publicity

Posters and programmes

Fund raising and raffle

Ticket sales

Stage management

Venue and seating arrangements

Audience attendance and distribution

Was the budget workable?

Front of House and catering

Photography and video

Costings and accounts

The budget will need special attention at the de-briefing meeting. It can help for an efficient assessment if those who have incurred expenditure ensure that all the invoices and receipts are gathered in promptly and if each individual completes a detailed break-down of costs involved before the meeting.

Estimates prior to the production can now be compared to actual spending. If the planning has been scrupulous, sufficiently thought through and expenditure well controlled, it may

well be that all the finances balance up, more or less, to reach the anticipated figures. Any significant anomalies should be carefully scrutinised to discover the reason for the figures being either considerably higher or lower than expected

If, after careful analysis, it is felt that the budget for similar subsequent productions should be adjusted, then make note of this clearly. Greater restrictions may need to be imposed on exuberant spenders – or a more generous approach made to a particular element. If, for example, the lighting has been criticised as being

Element	Comments	Suggestions
Script		
Auditions and casting		
Line-learning		
Cast reliability		
Rehearsals and schedule		
Sets and stage hands		
Lighting, sound, special effects		
Costumes		
Properties		
Music		
Publicity		
Posters and programmes		
Fund raising and raffle		
Ticket sales		
Stage management		
Venue and seating arrangements		
Audience attendance and distribution		
Was the budget workable?		
Front of House and catering		
Photography and video		

Planning ahead

pedestrian, this might be improved with a little more spending power!

Meanwhile ticket sales and income will also be evaluated, compared to previous productions and assessed against expectations.

Keeping clear financial records of each production in this way will contribute greatly to anticipating the costs of future productions more accurately and, ultimately, to profitable long-term planning.

Planning ahead

Keep everyone involved! The advantage of a series of productions throughout the year is that a wide range of abilities can be exploited and enjoyed, and more people given an opportunity to take part. Energies can also be channelled into new directions, thus keeping much of the membership busy once again.

A good mixture of production styles and cast sizes should be balanced throughout the year to reflect the needs of the membership and to stimulate your audiences.

The fun of a successful play creates its own energy. Try to keep the enthusiasm that this has generated alive in the society throughout the entire season of productions.

Intermittent productions

If productions are not continuous through the season, it may help to maintain the group's entity by meeting occasionally between productions. If the group stages only an annual Christmas production, for example, then many months will lie dormant between the final perfor-

mance of one show and the first rehearsal of the next.

Perhaps, to fill the gap and keep the group together, the society might organise theatre visits – both to professional shows and to other local amateur productions. Much may be learned from this. There can also be a series of workshops, several social gatherings such as garden parties or barbecues, play readings – or work parties to improve some aspect of the venue or staging. The most practical members might paint the backdrop, build new flats or steps, or varnish the stage while others tidy storage areas, sort costumes or mend props.

There can also be fund-raising events, such as race nights or discos – ostensibly to find the resources to pay for new equipment but also thoroughly enjoyable in their own right.

It is good, by some means or another, to keep open the lines of communication and to continue the friendships and the commitment established through the production.

Videos and photographs

Many groups reconvene for a viewing of the video of the production. A video party will provide the excuse for a welcome reunion – perhaps a few weeks later so that everyone has had the chance to recover their energies. This will also allow time for the video to be processed and edited – and for any still photographs of the production to be numbered, labelled, put on boards or inserted in an album, whatever method makes it easiest to take and process orders. Nowadays most of the film processing companies can provide an 'easy-finder', a sheet of

Photo order form					
Name			Telephone		
Film no.	neg no.	quantity	Film no.	neg no.	quantity
			Total quantity		
			@		
			Total cost		

Last Avening Players Hilarious Theatre Awards

THE 2001 L·A·P·H·T·A AWARDS

AWARDED TO

Sophie Selkirk

FOR

The best scriptwriter

Never has anyone made up so many lines on the spur of the moment!

IN

A NIGHT IN A BILLION

AVENING PLAYERS LAPHTA

I have been nominated for being

absolutely astoundingly brilliant!

IN THE 2001 PRODUCTION

A NIGHT IN A BILLION

Last Avening Players Hilarious Theatre Awards

This kind of party requires thorough preparation. The venue must have sufficient room to allow good viewing of the video for all – and plenty of escape areas should be available for those who do not wish to watch the film from beginning to end. There will always be those souls who drift in to see their own bits and then vanish back to the bar area, while those partners who have less interest in the proceedings may not wish to be imprisoned in front of the screen for an entire evening.

Preparation of food can be shared amongst the members to ease the load. Generally, each person or couple contributes appropriate wine, beer or soft drinks to share so that the host does not need to incur great expense.

Meanwhile the award ceremony needs careful planning, and the preparation of appropriate diplomas and badges to add to the fun. Make it as humorous as possible – and not too long. Always keep a record of who won what, as, although this is only a 'send-up', people can still be hurt if they feel they have been excluded year after year.

miniature shots of the photographs plus their negative numbers. This facilitates accurate ordering.

Video party

The video party may be given a theme. Any fancy-dress idea will usually appeal to members of a drama group and will set the scene for a really good evening.

It can also generate considerable interest and hilarity if the evening is turned into a sort of 'Oscar' ceremony so that everyone dresses in style and awards are presented. These awards can be very 'tongue-in-cheek'. For example, the presentation to the best scriptwriter might go to someone who could not learn the real script and kept making up new lines – while an award for bravery in action might go to the producer for his or her courage during that last dreadful dress rehearsal! The most promising newcomer, meanwhile, may turn out to be an amusing prop!

Theatre archive

Theatre archive

The following memorabilia should be collected:

Photographs of rehearsals

Photographs of the show

A group photograph of all members together to be taken every few years or so

Top copies of newspaper photographs

A video of each show

Sample copies of each programme

Samples of every poster and ticket

Newspaper cuttings

It is also important to keep the following:

Copies of the photographs of individual cast members as used for publicity purposes

Duplicate copies, and negatives, of all the photographs, in case further copies are needed

At least one clean copy of the script

(A complete set of play copies should be kept if these belong to the group but generally will not constitute part of the archive as such)

An annual update of the list of officers and membership

It is amazing how quickly the years fly by. There is a constant ebb and flow of membership. People move away or vanish from the scene; new personalities arrive; children grow up and suddenly are participating as adults.

Meanwhile, the ephemera of posters and tickets, press cuttings and the like become scattered among this mobile membership – and certain elements of the society's history are likely to vanish altogether unless a deliberate effort is made to gather together samples of everything right from the very first production.

The character of every group reflects its history. It is very important to create a solid permanent archive to record the story of all the productions. This should belong to the society so that it forms part of its heritage – a memory store, and often a useful source of inspiration and reference in later years.

In order to do this, the society must be prepared to fund the collection and house it safely. For example, although many members will generously contribute copies of their photographs, no society should automatically expect an individual who has personally paid for film and photographs to hand these over every time. Right from the start, the group must take responsibility for building up the archive, pay its way and make this policy clear in order to ensure that the archive material for each and every production is properly funded by, recorded by and held by the society.

Apart from a photographic collection of the show, usually the group will need to invest in albums or scrapbooks, files or storage boxes to house the archive. These records might be kept by the chairman or secretary and, to ensure continuity, passed along for safe-keeping as the officers change in succeeding years.

Postscript

So now the show is really over. Already the next production is taking precedence in the minds of those involved. In a happy and well-organised group, the transition will be smooth. The cycle of planning, rehearsal, performance and assessment begins all over again, with fond memories of the last play being overlaid by fresh enthusiasm for the new and exciting project that is about to begin.

In some cases where the schedule of productions is very busy, there may be a overlap; the paperwork and red tape, plus certain aspects of planning and preparation, have already begun before the preceding production drew to a close. In a large group, there may even be different teams of people manning alternate productions, or each team, perhaps, organising just one show a year. If this is the case, then it is even more vital that the groundwork of good organisation makes it a simple matter to move from one show to another, with nothing overlooked.

It is to be hoped that the guidelines, forms and checklists included in this book will enable the administration of any theatre group to be efficient, successful and enjoyable.

Forms for copying

Pages, 26, 80-81, 118, 144 and 147-152 have been cleared of copyright restrictions and these can therefore be photocopied for your own use.

USA
To enlarge a page of this book to 8^1/$_2$ x 11 inches put it on 115% enlargement

Europe
To enlarge a page of this book to A4 (297x 210mm – 11.75 x 8.25 inches) put it on 118% enlargement

Cue sheet   Page

Act	Scene	Page number	Cue number	Cue triggered by	Action

Stage plan – square

WINGS

UR	UC	UL
RC	C	LC
DR	DC	DL

WINGS

DOWNSTAGE
Audience

WINGS

UL

LC

DL

UPSTAGE

UC

C

DC

DOWNSTAGE
Audience

UR

RC

DR

WINGS

Audition form

Play | | | Date

Name

Name for programme

Address

Post code/Zip

Telephone home

Telephone work

Fax home

Fax work

E-mail

Mobile telephone

Height

Role preferred

comments

Will you sing?

Will you dance?

Back stage

which capacity

skills

Other

i.e. Is there a night you

cannot come to

rehearsals?

Costume measurements   Page

Actor/Actress			Character(s)					
Chest	Waist	Hips	Dress size	Shirt size	Inside leg	Shoe size	Hat size	
Outer arm	Underarm	Waist to ankle	Hips to waist	Neck nape to waist	Underarm to waist	Shoulder to ground		
Notes								

Actor/Actress			Character(s)					
Chest	Waist	Hips	Dress size	Shirt size	Inside leg	Shoe size	Hat size	
Outer arm	Underarm	Waist to ankle	Hips to waist	Neck nape to waist	Underarm to waist	Shoulder to ground		
Notes								

Actor/Actress			Character(s)					
Chest	Waist	Hips	Dress size	Shirt size	Inside leg	Shoe size	Hat size	
Outer arm	Underarm	Waist to ankle	Hips to waist	Neck nape to waist	Underarm to waist	Shoulder to ground		
Notes								

Actor/Actress			Character(s)					
Chest	Waist	Hips	Dress size	Shirt size	Inside leg	Shoe size	Hat size	
Outer arm	Underarm	Waist to ankle	Hips to waist	Neck nape to waist	Underarm to waist	Shoulder to ground		
Notes								

Properties

	Needed by page no. (in script)	Act	Scene	In stock	Buy from	Hire from	Who making	Set designer organising	Collect from	Who for or	OS / on stage	Checked and or ready	Cost	Returned

Useful addresses

UK

Copyright information

The Performing Rights Society Limited
29-33 Berners Street
LONDON W1P 4AA
☎ 020 7580 5544

Fibre optics

Par Opti Projects
Unit 9
The Bell Ind Est
Cunnington St
Chiswick Park
London W4 5EP
☎ 020-8995-5179
Fax 020-8994-1102

Gauzes

JD Macdougall
4 McGrath Road
London E15 4JP

Gobos

DHA Lighting
3 Jonathan St
London SE11 5NH
☎ 020-7582-3600
Fax 020-7582-4779

Blanchard Works
Kangley Bridge Road
Sydenham
London SE26 5AQ
☎ 020-8659-2300
Fax 020-8659-3153

Lasers

Laser Magic
LM House
2 Church Street
Seaford
East Sussex BN25 1HD
☎ 01323-890752
Fax 01323-898311

Strand Lighting Ltd
North Hyde House
North Hyde Wharf
Hayes Road Heston
Middlesex UB2 5NL
☎ 020-8560-3171
Fax 020-8568-2103

Libraries

Drama Association of Wales
The Old Library
Singleton Road, Splott
Cardiff CF24 2ET

Lighting, sound & special effects

Gradav Emporium
613 - 615 Green Lanes
Palmers Green
London N13 4EP
☎ 020-8886-1300

Gradav Hire
Units C6 & C9
Hastingwood Trading Estate
Harbet Road
Edmonton
London N18 3HR
☎ 020-8803-7400
Fax 020-8803-5060

Kave Theatre Services
15 Western Road
Hurstpierpoint
West Sussex BN6 9SU
☎ 01273-835880
Fax 01273-834141

Lighting, sound, special effects make-up and staging equipment

Stage Services
Stage House
Prince William Road
Loughborough
Leicestershire
LE11 0GN
☎ 01509-218857
Fax 01509-265730

Machinery

Hall Stage
The Gate Studios
Station Road
Borehamwood
Hertfordshire WD2 1DQ

Triple E Engineering
B3 Tower Bridge
Business Pk
Clements Rd
London SE16 4EF

Unusual Rigging
4 Dalston Gardens
Stanmore
Middlesex HA7 1DA
☎ 020-8206-2733
Fax 020-8206-1432

Paint

Brodie and Middleton Ltd
68 Drury Lane
London WC2B 5SB
☎ 020 7836 3289/3280
Fax 020 7497 8425

Party things

BGS
152c Finchley Road
London NW11 7TH
☎ 020 8201 9222
Fax 020 8201 9111

Projection

AC Lighting
Unit 3
Spearmast Ind Est
Lane End Road
Sands
High Wycombe
Buckinghamshire
HP12 4JG

Optikinetics
38 Cromwell Road
Luton
Bedfordshire LU3 1DN
☎ 01582-411413
Fax 01582-400013

White Light
57 Filmer Road
London SW6 7JF
☎ 0171-731-3291
Fax 0171-371-0806

Pyrotechnics

Jem Pyrotechnics and Special Effects Company
Vale Road Industrial Estates
Boston Road
Spilsby
Lincolnshire PE23 5HE
☎ 01790-754052
Fax 01790-754051

Le Maitre
312 Purley Way
Croydon
Surrey CRO 4XJ
☎ 020-8686-9258
Fax 020-8680-3743

Publications

The Stage
Stage House
47 Bermondsey Street
London SE1 3XT
☎ 020 7403 1818
www.thestage.co.uk

Publishers

Samuel French Limited
52 Fitzroy Street
London W1P 6JR
☎ 020-7387 9373
Fax 020 7387 2161
www.samuelfrench-london.co.uk
e-mail
theatre@samuelfrench-london.co.uk

Scenery & Fittings

Streeter & Jessel
3 Gasholder Place
The Oval
London SE11 5QR
☎ 020-7793-7070
Fax 020-7793-7373

Signs

Seaton Limited
Department AQ
PO Box 77
Banbury
Oxon OX16 7LS
☎ 0800 585501
Fax 0800 526861

Sound Effects Libraries

ASC Ltd
1 Comet House
Caleva Park
Aldermaston RG7 4QW

Digiffects
Music House (Intl) Ltd
5 Newburgh Street
Soho
London W1V 1LH

Stage Associations

National Operatic & Dramatic Association
NODA House
1 Crestfield Street
London WC1H 8AU
☎ 020-7837-5655
Fax 020-7833-0609

National Drama Festivals Association
Bramleys, Main Street
Shudy Camps
Cambridgeshire CB1 6RA
☎ 01799 584920
fax 01799 584921
e-mail
TonyBroscomb@compuserve.com

amateur theatre network
AMDRAM
http://www.amdram.co.uk

Stage Make-Up

Charles Fox
22 Tavistock St
London WC2

L. Leicher
202 Terminus Road
Eastbourne
East Sussex BN21 3DF

Theatre Zoo
28 New Row
London WC2

Textiles, paint & make-up

Brodie & Middleton
68 Drury Lane
London WC2B 5SP
☎ 020-7836-3289/80
Fax 020-7497-8425

Useful addresses

Further reading

USA

Blacklights

Wildfire Inc.
11250 Playa Court
Culver City
CA 90230-6150
☎ 310-398-3831
Fax 310-398-1871

China Silk

Horikoshi NY, Inc.
55 West 39th Street
New York NY 10018
☎ 212-354-0133

Copyrights

ASCAP
The American Society of
Composers, Authors and
Publishers
1 Lincoln Plaza
New York
NY 10023
☎ 212-621-6000
www.ascap.com

BMI
Broadcast Music
Incorporated
320 W. 57th Street
New York
NY 10019
☎ 212-586-2000
www.bmi.com

SESAC
Society of European
Authors and Composers
421 W. 54th Street
New York
NY 10019
☎ 212-586-3450
www.sesac.com

**The US Copyright
Office website**
lcweb.loc.gov/copyright

Costumes

Costume World
2200 NW 32nd Street
Building S, Suite /300
Pompano Beach, FL
33069
☎ 800-423-7496
Fax 954-978-8293

Fibre Optics

Fiber Optic Systems
2 Railroad Ave
Whitehouse Station
NJ 08889
☎ 201-534-5500
Fax 201-534-2272

Mainlight
PO Box 1352
Boxwood Ind Park
402 Meco Drive
Wilmington DE 19899
☎ 303-998-8017
Fax 302-998-8019

Gobos

Great American Market
826 N Cole Ave
Hollywood CA 90038
☎ 213-461-0200
Fax 213-461-4308

Rosco
36 Bush Ave
Port Chester NY 10573
☎ 914-937-5984
Fax 914-937-1300

Lasers

Image Engineering
10 Beacon Streer
Somerville
MA 02111143
☎ 617-661-7938
Fax 617-661-9753

Lighting

**Plazma Globes,
Crackling Neon**
Larry Albright & Ass.
419 Sunset
Venice CA 90291
☎ 310-399-0865
Fax 310-392-9222

Strand Lighting Inc
Second Floor
151 West 25th Street
New York NY 10001
☎ 212-242-1042
Fax 212-242-1837

Make-up

Theatrical Supply
256 Sutter Street
San Francisco
California 94102

**M Stein Cosmetic
Company**
430 Broome Street
New York City 110018

Projection

Optikinetics
Rt 1 Box 355B
Doswell VA 23047
☎ 804-227-3550
Fax 804-227-3585

Pyrotechnics

Group One
USA distributors for Jem
Pyrotechnics and Jem
Smoke Machines
80 Sea Lane
Farmingdale
NY 11735
☎ 516-249-3662
Fax 516-753-1020

Sound Effects Libraries

Gefen Systems
6261 Variel Avenue
- Suite C
Woodland Hills
CA 91367

**Dimension Sound
Effects**
27th Dimension Inc
PO Box 1561
Jupiter FL 33468

Strobes, Lighting Effects

Diversitronics
231 Wrightwood
Elmhurst IL 60126
☎ 708-833-4495
Fax 708-833-6355

Jauchem & Meeh
43 Bridge Street
New York NY 11201
☎ 718-875-0140
Fax 718-596-8329

For the latest books on
drama and theatre
contact A & C Black (UK)
and Watson-Guptill
(Backstage Books) USA,
who publish a wide range
of relevant books and will
be happy to supply
brochures and listings.

Campbell, Drew
**Technical Theatre for
Nontechnical People**
Allworth Press, 1999

Cook, Judith
Back Stage
Harrap Limited, 1987

Davies, Gill
**Create Your Own Stage
Effects**
A & C Black (UK), 1999
Watson-Guptill (USA),
1999

Davies, Gill
Staging a Pantomime
A & C Black, 1995

Dearing, Shirley
**Elegantly Frugal
Costumes**
Meriwether, 1992

Govier, Jacquie
**Create Your Own
Stage Props**
A & C Black, 1980

Govier, Jacquie and
Davies, Gill
**Create Your Own
Stage Costumes**
A & C Black, 1996

Hoggett, Chris
Stage Crafts
A & C Black, 2000

Holt, Michael
**Stage Design and
Properties**
Phaidon Press, 1995

Ingham, Rosemary
**The Costume
Designer's Handbook**
Heinemann, 1992

onazzi, Daniel A.
**The Stagecraft
Handbook**
Betterway, 1996

Kidd, Mary T.
**Stage Costume Step-
By-Step**
Betterway, 1996

Jackson, Sheila
Costumes for the Stage
The Herbert Press, 1988

James, Thurston
**The Prop Builder's
Molding & Casting
Handbook**
Betterway, 1990

ILebrecht, James and
Deena Kaye
**Sound and Music for the
Theatre**
Focal Press, 1999

Lounsbury, Warren C. and
Norman C. Boulanger
**Theatre Backstage
from A to Z**
University of Washington
Press, 2000

Peacock, John
Costume: 1066-1990s
Thames & Hudson, 1994

Peithman, Stephen and
Neil Offen
**The Stage Directions
Guide to Publicity**
Heinemann, 1999

Pilbrow, Richard
Stage Lighting
Studio Vista, 1979

Pilbrow, Richard
Stage Lighting Design
Design Press, 2000

Reid, Francis
The Staging Handbook
A & C Black, 1995

Streader, Tim and
Williams, John A
**Create Your Own
Stage Lighting**
Bell & Hyman
Prentice Hall Inc. 1985

Thomas, Terry
Create Your Own Stage Sets
A & C Black
Prentice Hall Inc. 1985

Young, Douglas
Create Your Own Stage Faces
Bell & Hyman 1985
Prentice Hall Inc. 1985

Reid, Francis
The Staging Handbook
A & C Black, 1995

Reid, Francis
The Stage Lighting Handbook
A & C Black, 1996

Reid, Francis
Designing for the Theatre
A & C Black, 1995

Shelley, Steven Louis
A Practical Guide to Stage Lighting
Focal Press, 1999

Swinfield, Rosemarie
Hair & Wigs for the Stage
Betterway, 1999

Swinfield, Rosemarie
Period Make-up for Stage and Screen
A & C Black, 1997

Swinfield, Rosemarie
Stage Make-up
A & C Black, 1995

Swinfield, Rosemarie
Stage Makeup Step-By-Step
Betterway, 1995

Thudium, Laura
Stage Makeup: The Actor's Complete Step-By-Step Guide
Back Stage Books, 1999

3D
Three dimensional or creating this effect

A dead
Predetermined position for a flown item

Acting area
The area of the stage in which the actors perform

Adapter or splitter
A means by which two or more electrical devices can be made to share the same power point

Aluminium
Aluminum

Ampere
A measurement of the rate of flow, or current, of an electrical circuit

Angle poise
Small lamp on an adjustable arm

Apron
Part of the stage projecting into the auditorium in front of the house curtains

Area separation
Dividing the acting area of the stage into suitable units that can be lit independently or together

Auditorium
The audience area beyond the stage

Backcloth
A scenic canvas or 'drop' used across the back of the stage, often serving as a sky-cloth

Backstage
The non-acting area behind the proscenium arch

Bar
Pipe or barrel above the stage for the suspension of lighting and scenery; may be called a batten

Barn doors
Four separately hinged doors on a pivoted frame at the front of Fresnels or PC's. These can be used to shape the beam and prevent

spill light Not suitable for profile spots

Batten
Bar from which lighting equipment can hang: also applied to compartment-type lighting or border-lights

Batten
Scenic wood lengths for tautening cloth at top or bottom or timber used to join flats

Boom or light tree
A vertical pipe which can support several luminaires on a number of boom arms.

Border
A horizonatally placed flat or cloth hung from bar or ceiling grid to mask lights and flown scenery from the audience

Box set
A room setting with only three walls

Brace cleat
Attachment on the back of a flat to which the stage brace is hooked

Braces
Supports, usually adjustable, that are fixed to flats. May be screwed to the floor but are mostly secured by weights

Castor
Caster

Centre
Center

Centre line
A line running through the exact centre of the proscenium arch

Chasing lights
Lights that flash on and off quickly in succession

Cinemoid
Cellulose acetate which is used to make colour filters in the UK

Cleat
Fitting on flats to which throw lines are secured

Cloth
Area of scenic canvas hanging vertically

Colour
Color

Composite gel
Different coloured pieces of colour gel cut to fit together into one colour frame

Control cable
Cable to connect desk to dimmer racks

Costumier
Costumer

Cotton
Cotton wool or cotton balls or a cotton fabric Also a sewing thread

Cotton buds
Cotton swabs

Cross plugging
A system whereby several luminaires can be made to share the same circuit or dimmer alternately or at different times

Cross-fade
To fade or change from one lighting stage to another

Cue
The moment at which a set, sound or lighting change will be initiated. The cue may be a line in the play, a change of tempo in a song, or a particular piece of action of stage - whatever has been entered on the cue sheet

Cue sheet
A chart on which all the lighting cues of a production are recorded and which the board operator or electrician will use

Curtains
Drapes

Cut cloth
Parts cut away for foliage effect etc.

Cut-out flat
A shaped flat in plywood or hardboard

Cyclorama or sky-cloth
A curved or straight backcloth hung at the rear of the stage. It is sometimes painted white and then lit as required

Desk or board
Controller for lighting racks. May also be used when referring to a sound mixer

Dimmer
A device which regulates the power in the circuit feeding a lamp, so as to alter the intensity of the light

Diorama
A scenic view or representation made with a partly translucent painting. If the light shining through it is varied, then the effects change

Down stage
Front half of stage

Dry ice
Frozen carbon dioxide which can be used to produce mist or steam effects

Earthing (grounding)
Means by which, for safety reasons, metal parts of electrical equipment may be wired to the ground

Elevation
Scale drawing of a side view of stage or stage unit

Feedback
The sound of the speakers is picked up in the mics and re-amplified. Early signs are a 'colouring' and then that only too familiar whistle! Do not confuse with foldback

Fête
ty or reception to raise funds

Fill light
Light which fills the shadows the key light creates

Glossary

Fish skin
Ultra fine 'fulle' netting

Flare
Usually refers to lighting spill, or can be spectral-flare rainbow effects

Flat
Standard unit of scenery with a wooden frame and canvas, plywood or hardboard covering

Flies
The area above the stage where scenery and lighting equipment can be suspended out of sight or 'flown'

Float mics
Microphones arranged across the front of stage

Floats
Area across the front of stage or lanterns used there, often floods

Floats or footlights
A batten of lights set at the front of the stage, which in historical times consisted of floating oil-wicks

Floodlights/floods
Fixed wide angle general spread lighting units, used for illuminating large areas of the stage or cyclorama

Floods
Floodlights giving a wide beam of light, sometimes ellipsoidal reflectors

Floor cloth
Canvas floor covering

Flown
Housed in flies

Fly mics
Microphones suspended - usually above the stage

Flies
The area over the stage itself

Focusing
In theatrical terminology, this does not necessarily mean achieving a sharp focus. Instead it describes organization of the direction, positions, shape, and cover of the beam - as directed on the lighting plan by the lighting designer

FOH
Front of House

Foldback
A signal through speakers or headphones to enable members of the cast, crew, band, etc. to hear whatever sounds that are necessary to enable them to complete their task

Folder
Binder

Gate
Aperture between the light source and the lens on a profile shutter; may have built-in shutters with which the beam can be shaped, as well as runners which allow for the insertion of an iris or gobo

Gauze or scrim
Large-weave cloth used for scenic effects which can be rendered either transparent or opaque according to the direction and intensity of the lighting

Gauze
Scrim

Gelatine/gel
A colour filter medium for lighting, which is made of animal gelatin; it is rarely used nowadays

Gobo (or cookie)
Template of thin metal with cutout design or pattern which can be projected; normally used with profile spotlights

Grid

Wood or metal flats bearing pulley blocks

Ground plan
Scale drawing of a set as seen from above

Ground row
Shaped pieces of standing scenery 60-90cm (2-3 feet) high

Ground-row lighting
Strip light lighting scenery from below; lengths of shallow lighting equipment or battens, for low-level lighting effects

Haberdashery
Notions

Hire company
A rental company

House bar
A permanent flying line

House curtain
The main curtain in a proscenium theatre

House
Everything beyond the stage

House lights
Auditorium lighting

Hum
A sinusoidal signal at a low frequency. Generally associated with mains frequency - 50Hz. An unscreened signal lead near to a mains cable or tranformer is frequently the cause

Key light
A light of high intensity, or the most dominant direction of light; the most imortant light on a set which focuses attention, such as moonlight through a window

Lamps
The high-power electric light bulbs used in theatrical lighting equipment

Left stage or stage left
The area on the left of an actor facing the audience

Leg
Long narrow strip of fabric. Black for

masking

Legs
Unframed scenery, canvas wings, or curtains which are hung vertically to mask the sides of the stage

Levels
Rostra, ramps and steps above the main stage

Lighting bar
Lighting or electrics batten, or pipe

Lighting plan or plot
A scale drawing detailing the exact location of each luminaire used in a production and any other pertinent information

Lines
Hemp ropes for raising and lowering scenery

Luminaires
The instruments, lanterns, or units used to light the stage; lighting fixtures

Magazine battens
Border lights or battens which are 'flown' above the stage (UK)

Mains operated
British term meaning electrically powered, using the 'mains' voltage at local or domestic level

Marking
Laying out coloured tape to mark the position of scenery

Masking
Hiding certain parts of the stage or equipment from the audience, using scenic devices

Masque
A popular court entertainment in 16th and 17th century Europe, performed by masked players and usually based on a mythological theme. It often included music, dance, and poetry, as well as spectacular effects

Master
A dimmer control (a fader) which controls other submasters, which in turn control the dimmers

Mic
Mike or microphone

Mix
A setting of the controls in sound or lighting

Mock-up
A structural model of the stage and set, often a forerunner to the final detailed model, made to scale

Monitors
Speakers, frequently wedge shaped, used to replay the foldback mixes

Mould
Mold

Music hall
Revue with old-time Victorian or Edwardian theme

Night lights
Small, squat, free-standing candles

O.P.
Opposite prompt or 'stage right'

Off stage
Space outside the performance area

On stage
Inside the performace area

P.S.
Prompt side - stage left

Pairing lamps
Joining more than one luminaire to one circuit

Panoramas
A painted cloth which can be wound across the stage to reveal a constantly changing view

Pantomime
English children's fairy tale production put on annually at Chrismas and the New Year

Patching
Using a cross-connect panel which allows any of the stage circuits to use any of the dimmers

Glossary

Pin hinge
A backflap hinge with a removable pin to act as a pivot. Two pieces of scenery may be held together using pin hinges. Each half of the hinge is attached to a piece of scenery. A loose pin is inserted through them both. The pivot action of the hinge remains unimpaired

Plot
General list required by all departments noting exact requirements and cues for the entire show

Post codes
Zip codes

Practical
A lighting fixture or property which is apparently used on the set by the actors during the production, and so is visible to the audience and must be operational. Can also mean any fixture or prop which is illuminated

Preset
A group of faders. Can also mean a pre-arranged lighting state being held in readiness for future use

Profile flat
Alternative to the cut-out flat

Profile spot
Ellipsoidal reflector spotlight; provides a soft or hard-edged beam of light focused by a lens system

Programme
Program

Prompt
Person responsible for prompting actors who forget lines: may also prompt technical cues

Props / Properties
Anything used on stage that is not part of scenery, wardrobe, light or sound

Proscenium arch
The stage opening which, in a traditional theatre, separates the actors from the audience: sometimes called the 'fourth wall'

Public house
Inn or bar

Pyrotechnics
May mean fireworks, but in lighting circles generally refers to any bangs, flashes or smoke that might be required

Rake
Sloped auditorium or stage to facilitate viewing

Raked stage
A sloping area of stage which is raised at the back (up stage) end

Returns
The number of routes from mixer to stage/amplifiers

Rig
The lighting construction or arrangement of equipment for a particular production

Risers
The vertical part of a step

Roller
Mechanism for hanging canvas cloth

Rostrum
A platform

Roundel
Can mean a coloured glass filter used on striplights. In the historical circumstances, it refers to a small circular window or niche

Run-through or run
Seeing a performance of a play (or one aspect of it, such as lighting) all the way through, from beginning to end

SCR
Abbreviation for a silicon-controlled rectifier; a solid state semi-conductor device which operates as a high-speed switch and is used in dimmers

Scrim
See gauze

Set
To prepare the stage for all the scenery and furniture used

Shutters
Part of a luminaire which determines the profile of the beam and can be used to prevent lighting spill on the edges of the stage or set

Sightlines
Imaginary lines drawn from the eyes of the audience to the stage, to determine the limits of stage which will be visible from the auditorium

Sky-cloth
See Cyclorama

Specials
Any light which is used for a special purpose or isolated moment in a production rather than being used for general area lighting

Spill light
Unwanted light which spills over its required margins or shows through a gap

Spot bar
Batten or pipe on which spotlights are hung

Stage cloth or drop
A vertical area of painted canvas which can be a backcloth, front cloth, or drop cloth, depending on its position on the stage

Stage left
Left to the actor when facing the audience

Stage right
Right to the actor when facing the audience

Strike the set
Dismantling scenery

Strike
To remove. The opposite of set

Tab
Curtain - front tabs are the main house curtains

Tabs
Stage curtains across proscenium arch

Throw distance
Distance between a luminaire and the area on the stage that it will light

Thrust stage
A stage which is surrounded by the audience on three sides

To fly
To suspend in the air

To focus
To 'set' the lantern directions, beam spread, beam shaping and, with profile spots, the sharpness of the beam edge

To mix
To operate the mixer desk

To plot
To make notes of level setting, cue points, cue times, etc. Applies equally to lighting and sound notes

Tormentors
Masking flats angled up stage and set at the edge of the proscenium

Trap
A door in the stage floor of large theatres, used for special effects and entrances

Traverse
Tabs set on a track across the stage

Trim
Scenery or masking hanging parallel to the stage

Truck or wagon
A mobile platform for scenery

Up stage
Rear half of stage. The area of the stage furthest from the audience

UV
Ultra Violet. Available in flood and strip versions. Must not be dimmed! At is most effective when used with care and UV paint

Volt
A unit measurement of electrical pressure between two points in a single circuit

Wagon
See Truck

Wing curtains
The soft masking of the wing space

Wings
The area to either side of the acting area

Wipe track
A single tab track, usually full stage width

Index

Index

Acknowledgements

The author wishes to thank Samuel French Ltd for permission to include extracts from their *Guide to Selecting Plays for Performance*.

Thanks are also due to Pontypool Players, Cowbridge Amateur Dramatic Society, Minchinhampton Players, *The Stroud News and Journal* and *The Citizen* for photographs – and, in particular, to The Avening Players for so many photographs, printed matter and for being the willing victims through whom the author's production techniques were largely practised and learned.

Thanks too to David Playne for lending his graphic design skills over the years to theatrical form creation!